Bluffer's ®
GUIDE TO
SEX

REBECCA NEWMAN

**Previous edition by
Sarah Brewer and Tim Webb**

© Haynes Publishing 2019
Published January 2019

A CIP Catalogue record for this book
is available from the British Library.

ISBN: 978 1 78521 619 0 (print)
       978 1 78521 622 0 (eBook)

Library of Congress control no. 2018960006

Published by Haynes Publishing,
Sparkford, Yeovil, Somerset BA22 7JJ
Tel: 01963 440635
Int. tel: +44 1963 440635
Website: www.haynes.com

Printed in Malaysia.

Series Editor: David Allsop.

CONTENTS

Neither the lack of seductive prowess nor the simple desire to avoid sharing sheets or bodily fluids need prevent you from engaging in that endlessly enjoyable pastime – talking about sex.

THE POWER OF LOVE

Sex – it's a powerful thing. Right this minute, hundreds of millions of people are actively engaged in it (give or take a few million). And that's not counting the ones actively engaged in it on their own. What Mae West called 'emotion in motion', and Sophia Loren* once described as 'like washing your face – just something you do because you have to', sex is all around us. The theme of countless songs, books, poems, films and plays, it is the hook which sells – well, pretty much anything really.

Sex drives us. It makes us – and, for the over-ardent yet deliciously happy departing soul, it sometimes finishes us too. It is a vast source of global pleasure. Unusually, it even has the pleasing advantage of being relatively inexpensive, since the basic equipment is free.

All of that said, there are many reasons why you might not wish to actually engage in it. Lovemaking can

---

* Sophia Loren is also quoted as saying: 'Sex appeal is 50% what you've got and 50% what people think you've got.' A girl after our own heart then.

be a sticky and time-consuming business. Some people might agree with the 1980s singer Boy George, who said he would rather have a cup of tea. Some may sadly be unable to persuade anyone else to join them in the act of conjugation. However, neither the lack of seductive prowess nor the simple desire to avoid sharing sheets or bodily fluids need prevent you from engaging in that endlessly enjoyable pastime – talking about sex.

In fact, abstinence may even afford some kind of advantage: you are less likely to find your life complicated by having to avoid divulging details of sleeping with someone you're not supposed to, or worrying about a curious growth on a part of your anatomy that you cannot mention in polite company. But articulated with panache, there's no better subject than sex with which to hook your audience, and no more diverse and exciting arena in which to profess expertise.

With such a fascinating subject, however, there are going to be those who think they know more than you do. If you are going to outshine them, you'll need a generous dose of detail, wit and insight.

This short but definitive guide sets out to lead you through the main danger zones encountered in discussions about sex and to equip you with a vocabulary and evasive technique that will minimise the risk of being rumbled as a bluffer*. It will give you a few easy-

* Gender matters. It is necessary to make quite clear that wherever in this book 'the bluffer', i.e., you, is referred to as 'he', it is for reasons of grammatical convenience. It is not for one second designed to be sexist or to suggest that men are more likely than women to be all mouth and no trousers. Not at all.

to-learn tips and techniques that might even allow you to be accepted as a sexual expert of rare ability and experience. But it will do more. It will give you the key to the ultimate bluff: how to impress legions of marvelling listeners with your knowledge and insight – without anyone discovering that until you read it you probably didn't know the difference between a Yab Yum and a Yoni. In fact, you will be a respected fount of knowledge about where to put what, commanding the rapt attention of your audience as you gently explain 'how to do it'. You will also come away with intriguing *aperçus* into sexual depravity over the years, the ammunition to describe the perfect seduction, and information to help you avoid the more unpleasant consequences of sexual recklessness.

So good luck and bon voyage. It is going to be something of a ride – better, perhaps, than the real thing.

Da Vinci would undoubtedly have made better use of the navel.
Maybe he did. It might explain the smile on the **Mona Lisa.**

MAPPING IT OUT

GPS navigation devices are all very well, but they do nothing to help us find our way around the human anatomy. In order to pass yourself off as any kind of sexual expert, an understanding of what connects to what is a prerequisite.

A cursory look at the design and anatomical positioning of the male and female sexual organs shows that when God designed *Homo sapiens,* aestheticism and ease of access were not high on the job description. The human genitalia are not exactly user-friendly.

It is interesting to speculate how more secular engineers might have tackled the task. Brunel, for example, would have foreseen the mechanical stresses which the male's thrusting action places on an already overloaded spinal column.

Da Vinci would undoubtedly have made better use of the navel. Maybe he did. It might explain the smile on the *Mona Lisa*. Madonna certainly understands its erotic potential, once revealing: 'When I stick my finger in my belly button, I feel a nerve in the centre of my body shoot up my spine.'

THE MALE

THE PENIS

A subject which, for all its gimlet-eyed prominence, not all men get to grips with – at least not in a way that can be shared in polite company.

The penis is known by dozens of pseudonyms, none of which is half as funny as the puritanically po-faced word 'penis' itself. It is one of the Creator's better jokes that the straggling, fleshy afterthought which hangs from a man like the knotted rubber blow-hole on a half-dead Boxing Day balloon is the tool by which he shall reproduce his own kind.

The human penis is the largest of any living primate and, unlike in the males of certain species such as bears, rats and dogs, has evolved without the need for a strengthening bone. The key to the design is the use of an inflatable bung. Having a dual function is not easy for an organ but the bung makes this possible. Although the flaccid penis is mostly used for urinating, simultaneous ejaculation is highly unlikely – because as soon as the male is sexually stimulated the inflatable bung fills up with blood. The organ then expands, stiffens and, as if by magic, the draining mechanism is cut off – sustaining the erection – such that its original urinary function becomes seriously impaired. In fact, this amazing bioengineering means the penis has its own hydrostatic skeleton – a method of support also relied on by lower life forms, such as, er…the garden earthworm.

The average size of the erect penis is 6.3in (16cm) when measured from tip to base with a straight ruler on the side with the wiggly vein. The variation in size is far less than the column inches devoted to it might suggest, with 90% of all men falling between the extremes of 5.6 and 7in (14.5 and 17.5cm) – and the bluffer tending to fall in the upper echelons of that range, naturally.

Claims on the walls of public conveniences throughout the Western world may be safely ignored, although the longest authentically recorded erect penis measured an impressive 13.5in (34cm) long and 6.25in (16cm) in circumference. That's longer than your average wine bottle, though arguably less useful.

Commiserations should be extended to anything under 5in. As for the length of the smallest human penis in the world? Pretty small. Anything measuring less than three-quarters of an inch is known as a 'micropenis', but some are still smaller than that. In some cases the body of the penis can be totally absent, in which case there might be a genuine case for specialist construction (or reconstruction) surgery, known as 'phalloplasty'. This is also a growth area in cosmetic surgery.

Interestingly, many men have a pet name for their penis; they don't like to feel that a stranger is doing all their thinking.

THE TESTICLES

The hairy twin gonads nestling comfortably at the base of a man's shaft are named literally 'the witnesses', a

Latin joke foisted on the world by prudish medieval wits of the medical profession. More recent descriptions you may – or may not – choose to draw on include 'the two veg to his meat', 'the colonels to his general', 'the coconuts flanking his palm tree', 'the potatoes to his beef bayonet'... (we could go on, but this is a serious treatise on sexual bluffing). Most simply, testicles are known in almost every culture as 'balls', though until the invention of the game of rugby, the synonym was slightly inaccurate as the organs are egg-shaped.

Q: What do you have when
you have two balls in your hand?
A: His undivided attention.

While the penis takes most of the limelight, the testes do most of the serious work, churning out sperm by the billion and regulating the outflow of minuscule amounts of 'sex drive' hormones into the blood.

Romantic lovers might work best in the warm, but the testes work best when cooler than inside the body, which explains why they hang down from the body in an adjustable bag.

In the Middle Ages, men drew attention to their genitals by wearing a codpiece ('cod' is Middle English for 'scrotum') stuffed with sawdust or cloth to exaggerate the size of their equipment. Contemporary ballet dancers do much the same.

Aspiring experts should also be aware of the perineum – that's the stretch of skin between the scrotum and the anus. The sensitive region is known in Chinese as Hui Yin, 'the gate of life and death', perhaps because when caressed appropriately it very powerfully encourages male climax, but when pressed firmly, has the effect of delaying it (aka the 'Chinese Squeeze').

THE P-SPOT

No, not the dot sometimes put in urinals to encourage better aim. In fact, this is the male sensory hotspot better known as the prostate. No matter what his personal feelings on the matter, the worldly bluffer must be conversant with the fact that it is not merely the more fragrant half of the species who get to have sensational hotspots. Advanced lovers are party to the fact that men do too, though their location means not all people wish to don the gloves and explore them.

Happily, merely knowing the name of the P-spot is likely to be sufficient. If, however, you wish to amaze people with the extent of your knowledge – as you should – you could add such details as: it is somewhere 'up there' or otherwise 'down there' (referring to the back passage) and that tickling it with a fingertip can exponentially increase the intensity of male orgasm (unless it is approached by anyone in need of a manicure, which is likely to have a rather less enjoyable effect).

THE FEMALE

THE BREASTS

Poets, lovers, poetic lovers and, let's be frank, most men have been known to become transfixed by the female chest (and have been as long as there's been one). While it might not be advisable to comment directly about a particularly impressive example, bluffers should never be afraid to speak admiringly of breasts more abstractly and lyrically.

You might – with a distant look in your eye – choose to invoke Robert Herrick, the 17th-century English poet (once condemned for 'obscenities') who wrote a verse 'Upon Julia's Breasts' begging her to:

Display thy breasts, my Julia, there let me
Behold that circummortal purity;
Between whose glories, there my lips I'll lay,
Ravished in that fair Via Lactea.

You might also repeat the Arab proverb that 'paradise can be found on the back of horses, in books, and between the breasts of women'. Whatever you do, know that while gifted lovers will be terrifically keen on cleavage, a man will never actively peer at it while holding forth on its magic. This goes without saying.

Breast size is determined by genetic endowment and something complicated happening with one's hormone levels around the time of adolescence.

There is strong evidence that an obsession with mammary tissue evolved before we'd washed off the primeval slime. However, unlike rounded haunches and slender legs, breasts are rarely, if ever, acknowledged as being sexually appealing in either the Bible or the Koran.

There is no doubt that breast size and shape are subject to changing fashion. Pity the poor women born during the Second World War. In 1963 large breasts were compulsory, by 1967 they had to be free of bras and by 1969 (in a return to the days of 'the flapper') they had to have disappeared altogether.

Males obsessed with breast size are advised to visit a Freudian psychoanalyst specialising in Oedipal conflicts. Or Las Vegas.

Maximum bluffing value In the mid-20th century, American tycoon Victor Kiam, then executive vice-president of marketing for Playtex, described bra sizes as: 'Ping Pong, Ding Dong, King Kong and Holy Cow!'

THE VULVA

The vulva is the name for the external female genitals, aka 'bearded oyster', 'cha-cha', 'poontang' and – for the geographically minded – 'The Grand Canyon'. Every bluffer will need to be clear that it comprises:

• the clitoris at the front (much like a bald man in a boat)

• the vaginal entrance (*see* below)

- two outer, fleshy, folds of skin (labia majora)

- two smaller, inner lips (labia minora).

It is widely believed women wear red lipstick and pout as a subliminal reminder to men of the existence of the labia minora. As if they could ever forget.

THE VAGINA

The name for the internal part of a woman's genitalia was derived from the Latin word for the scabbard in which a Roman legionnaire stuck his sword. Primmer types with interior-design aspirations are more likely to refer to it as 'the front passage'.

Q: What's the difference between a G-spot and a golf ball? A: A man will spend 20 minutes looking for a golf ball.

In fact, it is not so much a passage as a cul-de-sac, with a tiny exit at the top end into the neck (cervix) of the usually disinterested and intransigent womb (uterus). At rest, the corrugated front and back walls of the vagina are usually in contact to form an H-shape in cross-section.

These corrugations give the vagina a deceptively large surface area that allows it to expand significantly. During childbirth it expands to a diameter of at least 10cm, enough for a full-term baby to pass through. So you can shoot down any man who boasts he is 'too big' for his partner.

THE G-SPOT

Somewhere up there with the order of the chicken and the egg, the existence of the G-spot is one of those subjects which has provoked rather more debate than seems strictly necessary. For some time scientists attempted to locate it in human cadavers, an utterly thankless task given how few men can find it with the help of its living owner.

The facts you will want at hand are:

1. It was named after German gynaecologist Ernst Gräfenberg, who during research in the 1940s, found that an area the size of a 50p coin on the top wall of the vagina swells during arousal.

2. If pressed with the correct tempo, this area can reduce many women to crying, delirious, ecstatic frenzies (a similar effect to shopping at a Bond Street jeweller, but which can be done day, after day, after day, with no lasting damage to a bank account).

3. It can be summoned to life with a beckoning motion of the finger(s).

During the last decade there was a worrying fashion for G-shots, in which collagen was injected into the G-spot.

In its early days, claims were made that it multiplied pleasure, and eager fans – or at any rate eager journalists – called it the catchy 'party in a needle'. The risk of permanently numbing all sensation means that the only G-shot you are likely to encounter today involves gin.

THE OTHER SPOTS

U-spot Another term for a woman's urethra, or specifically the sensitive area surrounding the urethra mouth. That would be, er, where the wee comes out.

E-spot Term coined to describe the area of the female body which includes the G-spot and the surrounding Skene's glands, which, when stimulated with appropriate pressure, can lead to female ejaculation. (Male bluffers please take note.)

A-spot This has been used to refer to a sensitive zone in the female genitalia located between the cervix and the G-spot. Given a suitably receptive audience you might describe it as 'between the Z-spot and the B-spot'. This calls for bluffing skills of the highest order, bearing in mind that neither Z- or B-spots have yet entered the sexological lexicon.

OTHER EROGENOUS ZONES...

Both men and women are blessed with parts of their superficial anatomy which are more sensitive than other bits to stroking, kissing and other tender attentions. These are referred to as erogenous zones. Not surprisingly, they lie in places where you are not likely to be touched during the course of a day's normal social interaction (well, one would hope not).

Diagrams of the more esoteric erogenous zones are available from most disreputable bookshops. Take the view that it is better to ignore them and go exploring on your own over each new pasture that comes your way. After all, partners vary.

Earlobes, breasts, necks and anywhere within 15cm of the sexual apparati are usually good bets. Navels, backs of knees and tips of toes (once boots are removed) are long shots but can be astoundingly effective.

Anybody who honestly believes that saying: 'Hey babe, there's a party going on in my pants. You're invited' works, is unlikely to enjoy much success as a seducer.

SEDUCTION

An understanding of the fundamental principles of seduction is, as you might imagine, of paramount importance in the great game of *amore*.

While you must make your own judgement about the extent to which you choose to portray yourself as an expert seducer, any pretence to erotic aptitude must be grounded on a solid grasp of how to scale the foothills of seduction to reach the summit of the mound of Venus, or how to tackle the mighty heights of Priapus (another classical reference involving the Greek god of health and fertility, who from all accounts, sported something of a whopper).

FLIRTING

The art of flirting requires an intangible quality called charm, which comes naturally to some and tends to elude others. But rest assured that it can nonetheless be acquired (to a greater or lesser degree). There is one simple rule: make the object of your attention feel that there is nobody else at that moment whose company you would prefer to share. Make it clear that you are interested in him/her as a person, and that a distinct possibility exists that you might even admire his/her mind. Ask questions, and express profound interest in the answers. It is the basis of all flirting (and good flirts are usually presumed to be fairly proficient in most other relevant departments).

Handled by a gifted bluffer, the art of flirting conveys (by the subtle deployment of gesture and glance) the following messages:

a) I find you exceedingly attractive…

b) If things were different, I'm sure we could make the most wonderful love together (in a lovely hotel, no complications, plenty of champagne, etc).

c) But since neither of us is free…

d) Please accept my admiration instead. (Repeat a) if necessary.)

Depending on what happens next, a flirtation might develop into a full-blown seduction by turning a compliment into a proposition. For example: 'Well, we've established that we find each other unbelievably attractive. So let's see each other again.' Or: 'Any chance of losing your wife/husband/insignificant other for an hour or so?' Note, however, that these questions are never actually asked. They are hinted at, and much use is made of eyes and innuendo.

Studies have shown that up to 80% of communication between two people who are sexually interested in each other is non-verbal. After a few years of marriage, this figure can rise to 100%, whether sex is on the menu or not.

The key word to remember when trekking in the foothills of flirtatiousness is 'humour'. This is particularly true if you are a male seducer. Research has shown that men, when asked what they think women find attractive in a potential partner, place physical looks far too high up the list, and forget that for most women the ability to make them laugh is a key component of any successful seduction. But this must be achieved in the correct manner. It's about engaging in witty rejoinders, with an emphasis on good-natured teasing. It is not about marching up to a woman and asking if she's heard the one about the nun and the courgette.

Apart from demonstrating a sense of humour when flirting, there are some physical things to be aware of:

Lower your voice The idea is that your target will lean closer towards you and that proximity will make the whole encounter more sexually charged. Don't overdo it though, or you'll make them suspect that you might be ill (not a good seduction routine). Also, remember not to deploy this particular technique after consumption of any dish with a high garlic or smoked fish content.

Mirror their body movements This is an acknowledged way of showing that you're attracted to someone. Mirroring promising signs such as leg crossing and uncrossing, chin in hand and head tilted, tracing a finger across lips, are all good ways of expressing your interest. Conversely, if you notice the person copying your movements, you can be moderately confident that he or she is interested in you. It's not a good sign if they put two fingers down their throat (and it's even worse if you copy them).

Brush their hand Take every opportunity to make contact when passing a plate or a glass of wine. Let your fingers rest momentarily on theirs. If they refrain from pulling away, it means they are welcoming your attention. If they flinch, you've got a long, long way to go.

There is a certain
novelty in making good use
of a stalled lift.

IMAGINATIVE LOCATION

Every seducer should hint at a ready list of ideal places for consummation of the act. You might never make use of any of them, but to drop them into the conversation at a suitable opportunity cannot fail to give the impression that you know of the 'perfect place'. Moreover, it will show that you understand the importance of imagination when choosing one.

Such places can of course be customised to your own circumstances, or more likely your needs at the relevant moment, but consider such venues as classic yachts, idyllic cottages (especially those close to the sea), country houses and châteaux. Hot-air balloons, ski lifts and theme-park roller coasters with names like Oblivion might show imagination, but they don't show much sense. Failing all else, there is a certain brilliance in making good use of a stalled lift.

RETAIL RESEARCH

Sometimes, making your target feel special is the most effective technique of all. Gifts, especially those which demonstrate that you have taken an interest in your target's personal tastes and passions, can lower defences remarkably effectively.

An element of cunning might well be required. A useful ruse is to ask the object of your desire for help – as every bluffer knows, most people love to share their wisdom and expertise.

If seeking advice from a keen shopper – for now, let's call her a woman – ask her to recommend expensive and beautiful items for your sister, and let her lead you to her favourite shop. The woman is not yet born who does not get a tingle from the word 'retail'. Shopping is an experience which the female psyche finds thrilling, tantalising and almost (this is why it is so valuable a tool for your purposes) sensual. As a prelude to seduction, it is nigh on unbeatable.

Note carefully the items she lingers overs and fingers lovingly, then go back and buy them for her.

If asking the same favour of a male, you will find that there are many subjects on which he considers himself an expert and qualified to advise. If he suggests that your brother would benefit hugely from a signed edition of William Boddy's *The History of Motor Racing*, rest assured that so would he. Buy it for him.

BODY LANGUAGE

Study your targets closely. Their attraction to you can be signified by a variety of movements, many of them completely subconscious.

When a man finds a woman attractive, the signals can include:

Standing with his hands on his hips. But if you're looking for this sign, be careful to ensure that 'hips' are in the plural. If he stands with one hand on one hip only, he's unlikely to find you, or indeed any woman, sexually attractive.

The 'cowboy stance'. The man stands with his thumbs hooked underneath his belt, turns to face you and pushes one foot forward. Of course, whether you opt to pursue an interest in a man who chooses to adopt the opening position of a line dance is up to you.

Spreading his legs slightly. The underlying message here is self-explanatory, but you should take care as there are times when this stance can be misconstrued. He may simply be trying to keep his balance on a moving bus, he may be naturally bow-legged, or he might be Simon Cowell, in which case you may wish to reflect on your decision-making ability.

When a woman finds a man attractive, the signals can include:

Flicking her head to shake out her hair, or touching her hair with her fingers. Let's hope she doesn't have nits.

Sliding a foot in and out of her shoe. Very Freudian. Or else she is waiting to leave.

Sitting with one leg folded underneath her body, so that her knee points towards you. A sort of primal come-on, especially strong if she then leans her torso towards you. Crossed legs tend to represent the reverse – unless she is channelling an inner Sharon Stone.

Looking at you through lowered eyelids. It worked for Diana.

Letting her mouth open slightly, poking out the very tip of her tongue and gently running it along her teeth. Ladies, if you're intending to use this sign, be careful to keep it subtle. Otherwise you may dribble involuntarily, or look like you have issues with dental hygiene.

Signs of potential interest common to both sexes:

Showing the palm of the hand or the wrist. To reveal a part of your hand that would not normally face a conversational partner is acknowledged to be one of the surest signs of sexual interest. But again, subtlety is everything. Don't use both hands, otherwise it may look like they are open in supplication, or worse, in the universal 'weighing up' sign for 'I'm not kidding – they were this big'.

Changes to the eyes. When talking to someone who attracts you, your tear glands become more active and your eyes glaze over. There is also a tendency for your pupils to dilate, which some experts think is the body's way of seeing as much of the person attracting it as possible. You are quite literally getting an eyeful. Note, however, that glazed eyes by themselves could merely indicate he or she's about to fall asleep.

USEFUL CATALYSTS

Alcohol Always reliable.

Cake Equally reliable, except in the case of gluten allergy. Or a savoury tooth. In which case:

Cheese Particularly the melting variety such as Vacherin, which can be served baked. Sound surprising? So much the better, as it both works (assuming your target is *fromage*-friendly) and will provide 'evidence' of your unique erotic *savoir faire* to your enraptured audience.

Chocolate* A proven aphrodisiac (unlike that tired old cliché the oyster). The Aztecs, no strangers to a bit of hanky-panky, may have been the first on record to draw a link between the cocoa bean and sexual desire. The Aztec emperor Montezuma, who had 600-plus wives, was said to have drunk chocolate by the golden goblet-load to enhance his sexual prowess. It also lends a sense of occasion to the seduction routine.

MAKING THE MOVE

The actual 'pounce' can be done in all manner of ways. If we wanted to be gender stereotypical, we might suggest that women tend to flutter elegantly, and make him think he is doing the running, and that men might honourably wait for the 'signal' which, if not immediately forthcoming, can be hastened by assurances that you would never dream of behaving inappropriately or outstaying your welcome. If the hand isn't then squeezed, direct eye contact isn't made, and the lips don't part, it's probably time to leave.

At this point it might be a good idea to suggest that on those rare occasions when your seduction technique hasn't worked (we've all had our off days, or it might simply have been a case of bad timing), then your fail-safe fallback is a picnic in an imaginative location (if money is short) or a weekend in Paris (travelling first class and staying at the George V). If the object of your desire agrees to go, this old ruse is unlikely to fail.

OPENING LINES

It is a mistake to use hackneyed pick-up lines. Don't worry if you can't think of anything outstandingly original to say – it doesn't matter. Nobody ever came unstuck with 'hello' as a starter. And anyone banal enough to proffer: 'Babe, there's a party in my pants – you're invited' is unlikely to enjoy much success as a seducer. Leave clichéd remarks to those amateur seducers who buy books on the subject and practise in the mirror while flossing. Remember that the art of seduction is largely non-verbal anyway. (Having said that, there'd be something slightly weird about sidling up to someone and standing there mute.)

CLOSING LINES

As important as finding the way in, cultivating skills around the art of the exit is also vital. Get-out statements that have become dependable classics over the years include:

'My boyfriend has just gone to prison for GBH, so we'll have lots more time together.'

'My analyst wants to meet you.'

'Can you lend me £20,000?'

'I'd hate to ask you for a loan, but would it be okay if I used your flat as collateral?'

'I've taken the decision to accept Jesus/Allah/L Ron Hubbard into my life. How do you feel about that?'

'You really remind me of my probation officer.'

'I know that I'll only destroy you – and I think too much of you for that.'

'I feel that it's time for our sex life to move on to the next stage. You don't have a fear of snakes/spiders/rodents, do you?'

'Could you ever: agree to my mother living with us?/accept that I'm naturally unfaithful?/believe that herpes isn't always contagious?'

And the best of all…

'My wife/husband is threatening to leave and take the kids.'
This is an absolute winner, especially if it is the first time the other person has heard that:
    a) you are married
    b) you have kids
    c) he/she might be involved in a messy divorce.

Sex manuals have been around for 4,500 years but we are still chasing new ways of fitting a hopeful peg into a waiting hole.

TOOLS OF THE TRADE

YOUR BOOKSHELF

For as long as mankind has been doing it, someone somewhere has known how to do it better. This is as true of sex as it is of gardening. Sex manuals have been around for 4,500 years but, in the time we have made space travel a leisure activity and split the atom, we are still chasing new ways of fitting a hopeful peg into a waiting hole.

The trick is to compile a book collection which will do your bluffing for you. Any of the following will be a good start – and what you might need to say about them is duly summarised. Just remember to break the spine, so at least it appears that you have read them.

The Original

The Yellow Emperor, Huang Ti (also known as Huangdi), commissioned the first (nameless) sex manuals in 2600BC. These are the oldest such manuals in recorded human history. They describe techniques for kissing, titillating the erogenous zones and timing the pelvic thrust to maximum effect. The general theme was that a healthy sex life increased one's life expectancy.

The contents were advanced for the time and the marketing was inspired. The 'facts' were presented in the form of a series of conversations between the emperor and three fantasy women (the creator of *Charlie's Angels* may well have taken note).

Su Nu, the Plain Girl, was the clean, homely type. The Elected Girl was a flirt who rarely delivered the goods. The Dark Girl was the technical expert who taught the emperor – and thereby the reader – all manner of sexual tricks. Not surprisingly, this became cult reading and was considered to be a most respectable wedding gift.

The Jade Room

The most prolific sex manual compilers were the scribes of the Han Dynasty in the first three centuries AD. Their bestsellers were *Su Nu Ching* (*Lady Purity's Manual*), *Yu Fang Mi Chueh* (*Secrets of the Jade Room*) and various other titles on the theme of Jade. Amateurs often think that the Jade Room was a high-class imperial brothel. You will know that in fact it was highly respectable slang for the vagina.

Kama Sutra

Vātsyāyana, the fourth-century Brahmin priest who compiled the *Kama Sutra* would turn in his grate (he was cremated) if he could see what modern man has done to his encyclopædia. Sexual practice was certainly not its *raison d'être*. In fact the *Kama Sutra* was the equivalent of *Mrs Beeton's Book of Household Management*, a sort of yuppies' handbook for 1,000 years' worth of Indian social climbers.

While detailed sexual hints are included, they make up only a part of the central section of the book, which is told in 1,250 verses. Recipes for love potions appear but so do cures for spots. There is advice not only on such niceties as the eight different ways of biting but also on the four levels of kiss (moderate, contracted, pressed and soft). Varieties of moaning include the whimper, the groan, the wail, the shriek and the sob – as well as suggestions to echo a veritable ark of wildlife. Relationship pointers include qualities to look for in a wife – and how to choose the best extramarital liaison.

Its few dozen illustrated suggestions for acrobatic lovemaking are not drawn to scale – doubtless to encourage the eager sexual athlete to engage. The portly Westerner is advised to limber up a little before seeking to achieve penetration in many of the more advanced positions (though of course, by leaving the book visible on the shelf, the bluffer doesn't need to bother with these).

The Art of Love
Master Tung-hsuan, the seventh-century Chinese writer, was the first of many authors to say 'art' when he meant 'types', and 'love' when he meant 'sex'. In fact he had a way with words generally. Among the names he gives to the vagina are the Deep Vale, the Open Peony and the Chicken's Tongue. The male organ is referred to as the Turtle Head, the Swelling Mushroom and

the Positive Peak. *The Art of Love* illustrates 30 poses for keen contortionists and gives them wonderfully descriptive names such as Unicorn's Horn, Galloping Steed, Jumping White Tiger and the excruciating Flying Ducks Reversed.

Priceless Recipes

Sun Ssu-mo (or Tsu-mo according to other sources) was a Chinese court physician of the ninth century. His leaning was towards the philosophy of sexual practice and he was exceedingly smart. This is the chap to quote at dinner parties as none of your fellow guests will have heard of him. He is not to be confused with Sun Tzu, a philosopher and soldier, who lived about a thousand years before and famously wrote *The Art of War* ('every battle is won before it is ever fought', etc.).

Sun Ssu-mo held that after the age of 40, a man's potency declines and so he should learn advanced sexual technique while in his mid-30s. He believed that before that age a man was too ignorant, and after it too feeble, to understand what he was doing. Naturally a bluffer will not have this problem since, like a fine wine, his skills mature with advancing years.

The Book of Exposition in the Science of Coition

A bit of a mouthful, and lesser known (deservedly so), this book is by an obscure medieval Arab theologist. It was the first compendium of marital arts from the Middle East. It was also the first text in which the woman is seen as a passive object in a ritual which barely concerns her. Its opening lines are: 'Praise to the

Lord who...made the thighs of women anvils for the spear-handles of men.'

The Perfumed Garden

The original *Perfumed Garden for the Soul's Delectation* was written by a Tunisian nobleman called The Shaykh Nefwazi in the 16th century. It had an Islamic ring to it but lacked the misogynistic approach of *The Book of Exposition*. It opened with the far more egalitarian words: 'Praise to the Lord who...destined the natural parts of man to afford the greatest enjoyment to women.'

It is hailed as an erotic masterpiece but it is useful too. It includes a 'good woman' guide, outlining the sort of attributes a man should look out for in a potential conquest, and a 'good man' guide, detailing both the standard fittings and deluxe items available in a decent male.

The Joy of Sex

This 1970s classic is the million-copy bestseller of the modern sex manuals. Alex Comfort, its author, was a bearded guru who wrote simply and sympathetically about the troubles mortals have in keeping sex scintillating. The early Chinese would not be impressed by its absence of soul, but as a book for its time it reflects the sexual mores of the 20th-century practitioner perfectly – the 'suck-it-and-see' approach. Seek an original edition, in which the drawings also feature the luxuriant facial hair (mainly on the men) that continues to inspire fond devotion.

OTHER BOOKS WITH WHICH TO BLUFF

Lady Chatterley's Lover
DH Lawrence paints the exhilaration of love across the class divide, and among the marrows.

L'Étranger
There is nothing like a spot of Albert Camus and his seductive brand of French nihilism to voice your existential credentials and Gallic sex appeal.

The Road to Oxiana
Let this tome by Robert Byron demonstrate that you are both a man of the world and a lover of literature.

The She-Devils
Once you might have picked *Delta of Venus*. But any work by Anaïs Nin is a little hackneyed today, great as it is. A more elegant choice might be this bit of classic French erotica by Pierre Louÿs, in which a mother and her three daughters share sexual adventures with the same man, each other, and more or less anyone else they encounter. The redoubtable, if on occasion exhausting, Susan Sontag claimed this to be one of the few erotic works to achieve true literary status.

Song of Solomon
The Bible is a much sexier read than you might imagine. Solomon was not only famously wise and wealthy, he was also something of a sex machine, with a thousand

wives and concubines. In this text (also known as the Song of Songs) he collates some of the world's greatest love poetry.

Story of O
A groundbreaking work written in 1954 by highly sophisticated French journalist and author Anne Desclos (who used the pseudonym Pauline Réage) about love, dominance and submission. Feel free to point out that Graham Greene and Harold Pinter were both fans, and bear in mind you are signalling both a strong sense of sexual sophistication and a kinky edge.

120 Days of Sodom
A profoundly seminal work depicting scenes of such breathtaking depravity that it makes the most graphic online sex content seem positively mundane. State with confidence that its author Donatien Alphonse François de Sade, otherwise known as the Marquis de Sade, was unquestionably the foremost sex writer of the 18th century (and the 19th, 20th and 21st). Inform your listeners that he spent 32 of his 74 years either in prison or in an insane asylum. So he had a lot of time on his hands.

Justine
De Sade's other most famous work tells the story of a young maiden who we first meet as she pursues her quest for 'virtue'. Unfortunately she is unsuccessful, instead finding herself abused by a succession of men of the cloth, in some fairly unspeakable ways. (*Plus ça change,* as the French say.)

Napoleon called *Justine* 'the most abominable book ever engendered by the most depraved imagination' and promptly had de Sade banged up for the last 13 years of his life.

BOOKS WITH WHICH NOT TO BLUFF

Sadly, most sex manuals published since the 1970s smack of an overemphasis on basic technique rather than the accumulation of scholar-soldier-poet knowledge which owning older books implies. None of the former are useful to the bluffer, as they are designed for strict Tab A goes into Slot B explanations. Hence, you should never confess to having read them.

And neither should you admit to having read a book called *Fifty Shades of Grey* which you will dismiss as sounding about as erotic and instructive as the contents of your maiden aunt's lingerie drawer (which it might have been named after).

YOUR BEDSIDE

If you wish to be considered as a person who embraces, nay, straddles, the world of sex, setting the scene of the bedroom is vitally important. Of course, a mirrored ceiling or a rotating bed is wholly beneath one's dignity; ditto satin sheets (too Barbara Cartland) or suggestive Oo Er, Missus! artwork (too Frankie Howerd).

No, the items you will want someone to glimpse as they wander around your house should include: a proper robe, a mahogany chest of drawers of the sort that looks like it contains elegant and exotic items (as opposed to a hot water bottle, some cough sweets and a book of selected *Times* sudokus) and never, ever tissues. Cut flowers, yes. Candles, and in the bathroom great fluffy towels, also yes. Obvious displays of cuffs, canes, crops and whips – see below – suggest you're trying too hard to make your point, and can be nasty dust traps.

> Obvious displays of cuffs, canes, crops and whips suggest you're trying too hard to make your point.

Linen sheets with a high thread count (Frette, naturally), low lighting and sturdy headboard are more than enough.

YOUR TOY BOX

It doesn't matter if your idea of a sex toy is a Barbie doll in a bikini, or Ken in a mankini – the contents of your fictitious toy box need never be revealed.

Bluffing about 'vanilla' sex (which you will need to know is that variety which comes under the heading of conventional sexual behaviour) need not stray near the value of a deerskin versus a calfskin 'flogger', and need not trouble itself either with what a 'plug' might be, why it needs to be 'flanged', or what one might attempt to plug it into.

Accompany any mention of 'toys' with merely a knowing smile, or perhaps a look of 'darling that is so last year', and move on.

You should, however, have a passing acquaintance with:

The Pebble

Not something found in babbling streams, sadly, as these little marvels are roughly the same price as a bottle of Château Margaux. Rather, a small, rounded and easily insertable vibrator – which amateurs or the uninitiated might confuse with a stunted computer mouse.

The Rabbit

The world's bestselling sex toy is the rabbit, a vibrator which has a rabbit clutching, koala-like, the main shaft of the instrument. The idea is that the ears of the bunny will tickle the clitoris while the length of the toy ploughs, so to speak, the main furrow. A child of the 1990s, it became famous after appearing in the TV series *Sex and the City*. It has given a whole new tenor to the phrase 'rabbiting on'.

The Blindfold/Wrist Cuff

Self-explanatory. But you might venture that you prefer to use a Hermès tie or silk scarf rather than something as obvious as a studded leather cuff or blindfold.

ONE IN THE HAND (AND MOUTH TOO)

MASTURBATION

At least 90% of men, both single and in relationships, masturbate – and these are just the ones who admit to it.

It is not easy to imagine a situation in which a male would want to bluff about his manual dexterity when pleasuring himself; similarly, a female will rarely recount her own prowess at lending herself a hand. Rather, the key is to have a passing knowledge of the following useful gambits – knowledge of which will attest to your greater interest and expertise.

Sexual 'handiwork' has a strong, identifiable historical precedent. The Egyptians celebrated masturbation as the process by which the sun god, Aten, created the first Adam and Eve equivalents: 'With the hand of God, Aten masturbated and brought forth the first pair of souls.'

According to the Sumerians, who invented the first-ever written Western language, the Tigris river was created when the Mesopotamian god Enki masturbated, causing his seed to flood the earth. The Bible, however, takes a less forgiving view: Onan, who withdrew and spilt his seed on the ground, was struck dead. (*See* 'Coitus Interruptus', page 76).

For Him
At any given moment, many millions of men worldwide will be variously 'polishing the bishop', 'doing the knuckle shuffle', 'slapping the salami', 'spanking the monkey', 'tossing one off', 'meeting Madame Thumb and her four daughters', 'whipping up a hand shandy'… and so forth.

Today, masturbation is an accepted, if not entirely acceptable, pastime. Certain strata of society like British public school boys and American frat house college boys seem to derive particular pleasure from sharing the experience, and even emitting on to a cake or biscuit. The last to emit is obliged to…(well you can guess the rest, and it's not really a bluffer's territory).

The world record for the longest time spent masturbating for a male is held by Masanobu Sato of Tokyo, who, in 2008, masturbated for nine hours and 33 minutes. In 2009 he extended his record to nine hours and 58 minutes. One can only speculate that he might have been receiving personal tuition from that master of the tantric arts, the singer known as Sting. Admittedly, Sting has never proclaimed a particular interest in the more arcane and prolonged varieties of onanism, but one can't help but suspect that it's a subject on which he has interesting views.

The average number of times one man will ejaculate from masturbation in the course of his life is 2,000, assuming an average 60 years of sexual activity. That's once every 11 days which, on reflection, sounds like something of an underestimate.

Even as late as 1992, the entire concept of solo intimacy was considered inappropriate to address on mainstream TV. *Seinfeld*'s infamous episode, The Contest, cleverly broke the taboo by never once having any character utter the word masturbation, instead opting to refer to the activity using a variety of now-famous roundabout phrases like 'master of your domain'.

For Her

Even less commented on over the years, the world is gradually waking up to the fact that women also enjoy auto-stimulation. Again, a female bluffer will rarely need to share her putative skills on this, as the topic is not often, if ever, the subject of public discourse.

You will do far better to hint at your awareness by knowing that, while the advent of ladette-ism in the 1990s was the first time that women unashamedly confessed to resorting to manual pleasure, it has in fact been around a while. Cleopatra was thought to do it with a gourd full of honey bees (sealed, one would hope).

The 19th century witnessed the most surprising double standards. Everything was done to avoid accidental self-pleasuring: regulations were proposed which forbade girls from riding horses and bicycles because of the possibility that the sensations these activities produce might be enjoyable.

But, at the same time, doctors increasingly believed that the common female condition of 'hysteria' (anything from foot-stamping tantrums through to insomnia) could be treated by bringing a woman to 'paroxysm'.

In 1900, to speed things up in the waiting room, the Chattanooga was created and patented in the USA: a machine nearly two metres tall and requiring two men to shovel coal in a room next door, the working end was a mechanical vibrating arm which extended through the wall into the doctor's surgery where the appropriate genital massage was administered to the grateful patient.

To general relief, things became a bit more handy as time went on. The first cordless vibrator was patented in 1968, though it is only recently that all US states have finally legalised their possession and sale (except, possibly, Alabama).

One group which has positively approved the practice of digital self-pleasure in married women is the East African Muslim community. Apparently their logic is that only a superhuman man can cater to the sexual and emotional needs of the average woman and so it is perfectly healthy for her to lend a hand, as it were. Another recorded Western equivalent dates from the Napoleonic Wars, when French soldiers would give their beloved a dildo to tide her over until they returned from battle. And to think the French are hailed as romantics.

ORAL SEX

No one who wants to pass themselves off as a talented eroticist should be without an appreciation of the sensations which can be aroused by the giving and receiving of oral sex, described in *The Joy of Sex* as 'mouth music'.

These are the mouth-to-organ basics which you need to be familiar with:

FELLATIO

This is the acknowledged king of foreplay techniques, an art mastered by women with a glint in their eye and the ability to suck the chrome off the proverbial bumper (*see* 'Cleopatra', page 105).

Bluffers would be wise not to follow anyone attempting to convey oral proficiency by puckering their lips over a lolly or banana, by sucking languorously through straws, or lasciviously licking their fingers (though one could argue that a certain delectably voluptuous TV chef has based a career on doing this). Such amateur attempts are beneath you.

Rather, a skilled fellatrix can suggest her talents by presenting herself as a *bon viveur* who shows only the briefest tantalising glimpse of a flickering tongue as she savours a glass of fine wine or a chocolate truffle. And maybe, just maybe, she can demonstrate her ability to eat *linguine con vongole* without the use of a fork.

If recollecting great oral sex purportedly given, remember that fellatio is not location-specific, although it lends much more interest to the story if you come up with an imaginative venue. First-class flatbed on a flight to the Seychelles, yes; loo on a Ryanair flight to Alicante, no; the front seat of a Ferrari on a corniche in Cap Ferrat, yes; the back seat of a Vauxhall Astra in a lay-by on the A12, no…you get the picture.

Better, interest your audience in details of the history of the sport. Read on…

'Giving head' goes back to the mists of time. Indeed Lucy, the first prehistoric woman, is thought to have practised a sort of paleo-fellatio. It was also particularly popular in ancient Egypt, and notably practised by deities Osiris and Isis. The story goes that Osiris was killed by his brother Set, and his body was cut up into pieces. Isis found the bits and put him back together, but his penis was missing. An artificial penis was made out of clay, and Iris 'blew' life back into Osiris by vigorous attention to said clay pipe. Apparently Osiris was profoundly grateful, but it was never going to end happily. In fact they were brother and sister, and it all got terribly complicated. No wonder ancient Egypt went down the tubes.

The word fellatio derives from the Latin *fellare*, the verb for 'to suck'. A man performing the act is called a fellator, a woman is termed a fellatrix. The act was, however, considered taboo in Roman society, and was usually either performed by sex slaves or served as a punishment. For example, if a landowner caught a person stealing fruit from his orchard, he was legally entitled to demand that the guilty party fellate him. They had different rules in those days.

There is no Latin equivalent for the popular expression 'blow job', although *efflo opero* comes close.

The term is supposed to have a Victorian origin, as in 'below job'. It popped up in US vernacular in the 1940s where it entered common usage in the gay underworld. The act of fellatio then became a cultural cliché in 1972 when some amateur film-makers pulled together $25,000 for a movie that eventually grossed a reported $600 million. The film, starring Harry Reems and Linda Lovelace, was called *Deep Throat,* and the plot was as follows: a doctor discovers that his patient's clitoris is located in her throat and so helps her to develop her oral sex skills. Nobody was quite sure if it was intended to be a satire or a serious treatise on sexual mores, but it became a cult classic nonetheless.

Male chimpanzees have been known to lick the genitals of their female mates. But female chimpanzees have never been recorded repaying the favour.

Until 2003, when the US Supreme Court invalidated the old sodomy law, oral sex was illegal in 18 states of the USA, along with anal sex and various other 'deviant' sex acts. Fortunately for some, these states did not include California or Washington DC. Two notorious aficionados of the art include actor Hugh Grant, who was busted getting 'blown' by a street prostitute called Divine Brown on LA's Sunset Boulevard in 2007, and US President Bill Clinton, who had an unusually close relationship with a 21-year-old intern named Monica Lewinsky, between 1995 and 1996. Later, under oath, the president explained that his definition of 'sexual relations' excluded oral sex. Lewinsky had allegedly fellated the most powerful man on earth regularly for around 18 months – during which time Clinton doubtless did a lot of vital geopolitical soul-searching and not too much in the way of precision targeting with his chosen weapon. The encounter that famously left stains on her dress has been called the most lucrative blow job in history.

Do say 'I did not have sexual relations with that woman.' – Bill Clinton

Don't say 'The average man will ejaculate approximately one teaspoon of semen in a single orgasm (between five and ten calories). This does not explain why Lewinsky was a little on the chunky side.'

Maximum bluffing value When Clinton's memory proved hazy about whether oral sex took place, former first lady Barbara Bush is famously reported to have said: 'Clinton lied. A man might forget where he parks or where he lives, but he never forgets oral sex…no matter how bad it is.'

CUNNILINGUS
The more stylish bluffer will understand that the best way to approach a subject as delicate as the act of oral sex on a female is – obliquely.

Throwaway lines are good, such as this one from James Bond during a phone conversation with Moneypenny while in bed with his language tutor, in *Tomorrow Never Dies*:

Bond 'I always enjoyed learning a new tongue.'

Moneypenny 'You always were a cunning linguist, James.'

This sort of tongue twisting might help to convey the requisite skills involved in a good oral technique, particularly when related with a bit of wry eyebrow-raising. Remember that there are probably more people who can spell it properly than do it properly. Like most sexual skills, it takes practice.

The term is derived from the Latin words for the vulva (*cunnus*) and tongue (*lingua*), and is referred to in the poetry of Catullus and of Martial.

The act is accorded a revered place in Taoism. The aim of Taoism (see 'The Chinese', page 113) is to achieve immortality. This involves drinking from something called 'The Grotto of the White Tiger'. Quite why it is known as such is really for advanced bluffers only.

In Victorian porn it was known as 'tipping the velvet'; more recently you might refer to it as 'drinking at the Y', or 'eating pussy'…in fact you can make it up as you go along if your bluffing skills are in overdrive.

The missionary position has been around a great deal longer than missionaries. Male and female bonobo dwarf-chimps are fans, and so are armadillos.

FITTING IT ALL TOGETHER

Knowing little about positions but professing to have reached Casanova-like levels of sexual expertise is a bit like pretending to be Mrs Beeton without any obvious affinity with the most basic of cooking utensils.

Positions are the building blocks of the great act of lovemaking, and you might point out that the range of possible positions is nearly infinite. But while there are as many ways to sink a 'lingam' into a 'yoni' (it's a Hindu fertility thing) as there are ways to face-plant on a ski slope, there is a core of knowledge which you must be familiar with. You can, after all, only attest to your gymnastic deviation from the norm once you know what that norm is.

Note: If at a loss to describe a position you find yourself called to elucidate upon, any household or garden object – the screwdriver, the wheelbarrow, the corkscrew, the stepladder, etc. – can give it a name; indeed each of these already has, but no matter. As long as you pronounce it with sufficient gravitas, you will appear to be the master of it all. Try it. Ask, for example, in a tone of incredulity: 'You have never tried The Coat Hanger? My dear boy/girl...'

COMMON POSITIONS (MEN ON TOP)

MISSIONARY

The first and most basic of positions is the missionary. The male lies on top of the female in a more considerately braced version of a press-up position, and she lies beneath him facing up, ready to receive him.

A bluffer will explain that, as one of the more unreconstructed positions, it remains vastly popular due to its intimacy. The combination of eye-to-eye and full-body contact lend it to the sort of demure lovemaking scenes required by Hollywood – though because an audience can't see much, it is used less than frequently in the adult movie world.

Comments you should make will focus on this position's main flaw, which is the lack of stimulation to the female hot spots. You should therefore mention some of the add-ons and extras likely to please both parties.

These can be as simple as:

A cushion under her hips (details lend weight to your assumed insight: be particular that the best option is a stiff bolster, or a pile of Persian cushions, etc.)

Pulling her ankles up round the male back (if she is strong) or neck (if she is flexible) – both leading to the deepest sort of missionary stimulation.

The soles of her feet on his chest (also handy for kicking him off).

You shouldn't worry too much about the many variants of the missionary position. That said, there are a few which eager sex bluffers will be familar with – or at least the definitions of:

THE CAT
This is the missionary adjusted a bit. The coital alignment technique (CAT) has him shimmying up her body such that their bits rub together more usefully. Female readers of *Cosmopolitan* will recognise this one.

THE BENT KNEE
She places the soles of her feet on the bed, shortening the vagina and hence promoting stimulation of her G-spot. Easy, you can say with a flourish (it really is).

THE VIENNESE OYSTER
Her ankles are crossed behind her head. Not to be attempted if you've got a dodgy hip.

The term 'missionary', by the way, has nothing to do with Christian missionaries instructing natives that it was the only acceptable way to engage in sexual intercourse. This is a common myth given credence by Alfred Kinsey's *Sexual Behavior in the Human Male*. The word has nonetheless entered the modern sexual vernacular. Historically it was better known as the matrimonial position, and there is little doubt that missionaries believed that the alternative mating customs of savages were unnatural. Thus they vigorously promoted the man-on-top position, believing that semen needed to flow downwards for effective conception, and also – wait for it – because Adam was created before Eve, hence Eve should never be 'above'. This sort of religious logic is insurmountable.

The missionary position has been around a great deal longer than missionaries. Male and female bonobo dwarf-chimps are fans, and so are armadillos. Its use is depicted on ancient Greek pottery, and it is known that the position was favoured in ancient Roman, Aztec, Chinese and Japanese cultures.

COMMON POSITIONS: WOMEN ON TOP

These positions are generally very pleasurable for both participants: the male gets to lie back and enjoy both the ride and the view, and the female gets to choose pace, depth, rhythm and angle of penetration – all of which she is more able to do to assist her own climax, rather than that of her recumbent partner.

You'll need to be familiar with the following terminology:

COWGIRL
She straddles with her knees either side of his hips. Saddle, spurs and lasso optional (particularly spurs).

ASIAN COWGIRL
She squats, taking her weight on her feet either side of his hips. Especially memorable when combined with internal 'milking', using the vaginal muscles to massage the penis while riding. This technique is more commonly mastered by Oriental women, though it

is popularly believed to be the method by which the American socialite Wallis Simpson persuaded Edward VIII to abandon the British throne to marry her.

REVERSE COWGIRL
This is the one where she swivels round and faces his feet. When discussing this, a bluffer can state with conviction that it is to be favoured both in terms of physical enjoyment for both parties, and for an interesting change of scenery (for the male, principally).

The origin of the expression cowgirl is not hard to guess (just think 'bronco'). It is popular in porno movies (in fact it's practically obligatory) and is widely celebrated as offering a marvellously visual experience.

YAB YUM
A position which is a central part of the tantric tradition (*see* Glossary), in which he sits cross-legged and she sits cross-legged on top. Delightful for both parties and ideal for the lazy. The position can – you might choose to point out – be held for hours.

OTHER FASHIONABLE MEANS OF PENETRATION

REAR ENTRY
Universally better known as doggy style, for obvious reasons. It could, of course, have been called donkey style or goat style; fortunately it wasn't.

The position is beloved by those into deep, powerful

penetration – as well as professional footballers (most of whom know no other way) – and is usually carried out with some vigour. Done well, it lends itself beautifully to G-spot stimulation, and the kind of total-abandon-primal-screaming-wailing-banshee female orgasm which she will never, ever forget. Male bluffers please take note.

The male bluffer will claim to be *au fait* with the many slight variations. Naturally you'll know that from the common or garden doggy – her on all fours, you kneeling behind – there is a multiplicity of different methods of connecting two bodies 'from behind': her legs outside his (one can admire the added tightness), her legs straight and held up by him (a nice, advanced twist) or her upper back and face being pressed into the bed.

It is better done on a bed or cushion to prevent scraped knees, though you might allude to having used many different surfaces over the years – concrete, tarmac, sand, rubber, marble, vinyl and many others which can be adapted to suggest epic doggy endeavours. Otherwise, armchairs and sofas provide tidy support. There's also the popular 'desk-ender' if your thing is office sex, but bluffers would be well advised to be a little more imaginative than this.

FROGGY STYLE

She is flat on her face on the bed. You will, again, pronounce on the considerable improvement in mutual enjoyment that this position will provide when done with that firm bolster beneath her hips.

CUFFED
Her hands are knotted behind her, lending the posture a delightfully dominant/submissive twist.

SPOONS
Both of you lie on your sides, facing the same direction like spoons in a drawer (though, one would hope, slightly more animated).

STANDING
You might suggest this as a useful option when pressed for time or in a space where a) there is no cushioning or b) there is merely a doorway or alley or c) like Boris Becker, you are doing it in the broom cupboard of the appropriately named restaurant Nobu (after a courtship measured in minutes).

STANDING DOGGY
Can be done with both parties standing straight (*see* 'Bodyguard'), or more frequently with the female bending forward to clasp her ankles.

Not to be attempted by anyone who suffers from lumbago.

CLIMBING THE TREE
This is the *Kama Sutra*'s term for what we in the West call The Half Carry: you stand, and she stands facing you with one foot on the ground and the other curled round your hip. Anyone with a logical bent will recognise that in The Carry, you hold her weight. Bluffers should bear in mind that this requires a degree of practice and experience,

otherwise it might end in an undignified tangle of limbs and organs on the floor. Like most bluffing exercises, it is safer talking about it than doing it.

BODYGUARD

She faces away from him, standing straight. Nobody is quite sure why it is so-called because, frankly, it would be a surprising move for a bodyguard. But then since the eponymous film starring Whitney Houston and Kevin Costner, it seems one's duties go beyond opening the car door and batting off the occasional paparazzo. This, it would seem, is certainly true of the United Kingdom's female Home Secretary and her 'Specialist Protection Officer' in the BBC TV 2018 drama *Bodyguard*. The principal difference, however, is that the British bodyguard spends more time baring his backside than his American counterpart.

THE FLYING WALLENDA

A terrifying position named after a circus act involving high-wire acts and no safety net. You need know nothing more than the name (the reality is terribly confusing and deeply uncomfortable). You are advised to say sternly that it is not to be recommended, unless you're a trapeze artist.

THE INVERTED WHEELBARROW

An advanced version of the wheelbarrow position – man standing, woman face down with her hands on the floor and her legs wrapped round his waist. But (and here's the interesting bit) it's inverted…i.e., the woman is face up, her hands still on the ground and her legs still round his waist. She must be limber and willing; he must be strong enough not to drop her on her coccyx. Honestly, all things considered, you'd be better off with her reclining comfortably in a real wheelbarrow. (It makes gardening more interesting.)

VARIATIONS ON A THEME

Anyone affecting to be a seasoned lover should know that there are additional small touches which he or she might employ to add that extra spice.

Details you might therefore drop into the ears of your wide-eyed audience include:

TALKING DIRTY

You will recognise there is a whole gamut of good, clean, healthy, filthy fun to be had here. These days, lovers must be familiar with things like sexting – sending erotic messages over the ether, and the power of the stylishly edited video short. Skype or FaceTime have each done much to move the old chestnut of phone sex along, but a bluffer will do well to acknowledge the fact that dirty talk is an essentially risk-laden occupation – as one woman's response to 'you dirty vixen' may be quite radically different from another's. The safe bet, you might point out, is to confine it to the moment of sexual union itself and to whisper something really outrageously smutty as things build towards a crescendo. It does wonders to crank up the orchestra, and can be put down to the heat of the moment should it sound silly later. Which it will.

MIRRORS AND LIVE STREAMING
Have at the ready a couple of anecdotes of occasions, possibly in which more than one lover was involved, when the mirrors were arranged such that you seemed to be making love with an infinity of delighted parties.

A more high-tech approach would be to film it and play it back live – but best avoided due to a) the danger of high definition and b) the possibility of it being shared with the world (despite the millions it earned Paris Hilton).

Smearing trifle over your pride and joy while masturbating is not food sex, it's just weird.

OTHER APPROACHES TO THE ART OF INTERCOURSE

These will be covered in detail in *The Bluffer's Guide to Advanced Sex*, for there is vast insight that the seriously sexually inclined bluffer can share. For the moment, however, you will need to be aware of the following:

BDSM
Yes, BDSM. When asked what these letters stand for, you will patiently explain: Bondage and Discipline, Dominance and Submission, and Sadism and Masochism.

For the pedantically inclined the initialism should strictly read BDDSSM (but that is unlikely to be of interest to your audience). In truth, there is much more to be said once you reach the next level, of the various intriguing ways in which the endorphins can be played upon until participants are flying like kites.

Note: By now you will know that non-BDSM sex is known as 'vanilla' (after the blandest ice cream variety, with substantially less whips, clamps and fire tongs).

FOOD SEX

For now, you need only watch the really rather dreary and pretentious 9½ Weeks to get a grasp of the basics of simultaneously combining food and sex. But if you are seriously bluffing in deeper waters, stand out from the crowd by preferring sweet wine to champagne, and white peaches to the more ubiquitous strawberries. And note that food sex is something that should be enjoyed by two people: the ecstasy you might claim to feel when smearing trifle over your pride and joy while masturbating is not food sex, it's just weird.

WATER SPORTS, COPRO- AND NECROPHILIA

Trust us. You're not ready.

ANAL

A different approach indeed. For now, all you need to impart is that – done by anyone less gifted than you purport to be – it hurts like buggery.

Women are advised that physique and fitness are rarely determinants of sexual prowess in a man. Impotence is as common in builders, even bodybuilders, as it is in bankers.

HOW IT WORKS

All sex bluffers must have some idea of what is going on under the bonnet. It will enable you to impress your peers as well as reinforce your stories with perceptive biological insights. So, take a deep breath for the science part.

HORMONES

Hormones are remarkably clever chemicals which ooze into the bloodstream from a number of different glands. They can make the body do extraordinary things (aside from provoking pustular horrors on the faces of anguished teens, and turning the fairer sex into flaming, man-stomping demons every four weeks).

Female hormones come in five basic types, controlling fertility, sexual development, pregnancy, milk yield and, to a limited extent, sex drive and frumpiness. Male hormones are all variations on a single theme and control hairiness, genital formation, aggression and, to a limited extent, sex drive and grumpiness. All men have female hormones floating around inside them and all women, whether or not they wish to become Olympic shot-putters, have male hormones.

Because they are such subtle items, even the most biologically inclined bluffer need not bother to take on board much about hormones other than to respect them as being mind-bogglingly complicated and 'not fully understood'.

LIBIDO

The coy term for sex drive, libido is something an expert lover will (purport to) possess in considerable quantities; in mere mortals it varies enormously – from person to person and from day to day, if not hour to hour. The cause of sex drive is unknown. Women are advised that physique and fitness are rarely determinants of sexual prowess in a man. Impotence is as common in builders, even bodybuilders, as it is in bankers. Though the latter often have a notable supply of testosterone, they are still not immune to 'banker's droop' (limpness deriving from falling markets rather than sinking bottles of champagne).

Interestingly, the more sex a man has the more he wants. Not only that, new research shows the less sex a man has, the more he wants, too. Most men have a sex drive that is too high for most women; sex is always on the male mind, so their great challenge is to keep it in check.

PHEROMONES

These are one of the better discoveries of the 20th century, and can be harnessed to telling effect when recounting, for example, the time when you experienced that *coup de foudre* after merely scenting the back of a neck. The theory is that all mammals secrete tiny amounts which magnetically incense the opposite sex in a natural 'Lynx Effect'.

In the brief period since their 'discovery', these little chaps have been held responsible, rightly or wrongly, for sexual attractiveness, success at interviews, maintaining true love, goading tribal behaviour (such as football violence) and many other mysteries of the modern age. To a pheromone freak, kissing is clandestine sniffing, copulation is an orgy of aromas and Chanel No 5 is the social equivalent of mustard gas. Naturally the beauty industry begs to differ.

There may turn out to be a scientific basis to the claim that they affect sexual attractiveness. Wizened old lady chimpanzees who would normally have to make do with the odd banana instantly become the centre of virile young males' attention when sprayed with chimp pheromone. Ageing Hollywood sex symbols have been known to attempt something similar using musk oil and a splash of Davidoff Cool Water.

ORGASMS

Note that the plural is now in common usage.

When a man or woman performing a sexual act gets so far into the experience that their tubes go into an involuntary series of minor muscular spasms and the brain follows up with a sensation anywhere from OK to exsanguinated, the whole package is called orgasm.

It has been likened to ten sneezes happening all at once – which might be seen as a rather unpleasant experience (for both parties). A better and more traditional analogy might be the feeling of pure, boundless joy experienced when the in-laws leave after Christmas.

A man's orgasm, on average, lasts for about six seconds. The longest woman's orgasm ever recorded is one minute (something else women are better at).

Male orgasms are almost invariably accompanied by ejaculation. They vary in intensity but probably not in type.

Female orgasms are said to come in many different patterns and to consist of three distinct types – the clitoral (high-pitched, surface, buzzing fun), the vaginal (growling, deep, full-body roller-coaster fun) and the multiple (fun so good I'll be able to tell you about it on Tuesday, when I regain the power of speech).

Female orgasms normally fall into one of the following categories:

- The positive orgasm: 'Oh, yes. Oh, yes!'

- The negative orgasm: 'Oh, no. Oh, no!'

- The religious orgasm: 'Oh, God. Oh, God!'

- The faked orgasm: 'Oh, David. Oh, Thomas. Oh, Jim. Oh, yes.'

SPERM

Sperm is the male seed. Each spermatozoon resembles a microscopic tadpole. The average male ejaculate is 3 millilitres, or one level teaspoonful, and contains 300 million man tadpoles.

Sperms swim at the rate of 18cm per hour, so it would take them approximately 2,500 years to cross from Newquay to New York, if their average life expectancy were not limited to a long weekend.

They are remarkably resilient.

But perhaps not to the extent that they lend credence to the following popular story about an American Civil War soldier who was shot through the testicle by a bullet which then hit a young woman standing behind him. Both survived the unfortunate incident, but nine months later she gave birth despite protesting her chastity for all she was worth. It was believed that a small amount of sperm-containing tissue remained inside her when the bullet was removed, and this found its way to one of her eggs which it promptly fertilised.

Recount this if you choose to, but point out that it is a well-travelled urban legend known as 'the bullet in the balls' – sometimes advanced as the origin of the phrase 'son of a gun'.

Horst Schultz reportedly achieved a world record

ejaculation of 6 metres with a 'substantial' amount of seminal fluid. He also holds the records for the highest spray (4 metres) and the greatest speed of ejaculation, or muzzle velocity, at 42.7mph. Schultz presumably managed all of this without the help of a sexual partner, and there is little value for bluffers in maintaining that they could match his achievements (or even want to attempt to). Sex bluffing is not about distance or speed of ejaculation, especially when practised solo. But you might drop this sort of detail into conversation, just to show you know. Remember to shake your head in mystification about why anyone would bother.

OVARIES

It is this pair of petulant organs, connected to and below the fallopian tubes, which is responsible for spitting out a tiny human egg every month or two and manufacturing some of the hormones which cause a woman's premenstrual syndrome, postnatal depression, menopausal hot flushes, irregular, painful periods and, very occasionally, a normal menstrual cycle. All of these represent dangers to the male bluffer who must profess to recognise the signals and, if he has any sense, advise that every last and entirely reasonable request should be granted to the woman in question.

EGGS

A typical human female will be born with 400,000 follicles (potential eggs) already formed in her ovaries, of which some 500 will be released during her reproductive years. The ovaries take turns to release one egg each month – unacceptable in your average hen, but a fair rate of play in terms of creating human life.

FERTILISATION

The buckshot approach of the male seed-planter may appear to be wasteful but is necessitated by the awful inefficiency of the human reproductive tract. Any sperm making the distance is a hero of Herculean proportions, which makes every one of us heroes in our own right, and might be remembered in moments of despondency and low self-esteem.

To get past the cervix, climb up the uterine wall and find a fallopian tube, it must be armed with the physiological equivalent of an oxyacetylene torch, a set of Alpine crampons, several large-scale Ordnance Survey maps and a platinum American Express card. Once there, the chances of meeting a willing egg coming in the opposite direction, in the dark, are only around 1%.

Although it only takes one sperm to make a baby, the other 299,999,999 sperm in the average single ejaculate are vitally important to help talk that one sperm into going through with its momentous task. Even if fertilisation is successful, it is estimated that one in every three embryos is naturally miscarried within the first two weeks of 'pregnancy', without the mother being any the wiser.

LEVEL OF ACTIVITY

The philosopher Immanuel Kant died aged 80, unperturbed by the fact that his virgo was still 'intactus'. By contrast the late, great poet Sir John Betjeman was asked in later life if he had any regrets and he replied: 'I wish I'd had more sex.'

A bluffer, of course, will claim to know where to strike the right balance. While sexual inactivity can be a front for unacknowledged homosexuality, at the same time a few people simply do not possess a sex drive at all. For them, 'asexuality' is a normal state of affairs (or rather lack of them). At the opposite extreme, reliable research has found examples of sexually contented individuals who make love three times a day for decades. Bluffers will lean towards the latter tendency.

Men reach a peak of activity in their teens but, as they keep assuring themselves, make technical improvements well into middle age. Women reach both maximum revs and smoothest technique in their fourth decade. Unfortunately they are tilted off course by the menopause which has an effect on performance rather like that of an albatross being tapped on the beak by a Boeing 747. Fortunately the majority are adroit enough to bluff their way swiftly back into the game with renewed vigour.

ORIENTATION: HOMO-, HETERO- AND BI-

Most gays recognise their orientation at or soon after puberty. The simplest way to tell is to examine your fantasies. If they are gay then so are you.

We are all on a sliding scale of sexual orientation: only 4% of men and some 2–3% of women are exclusively or nearly exclusively homosexual. Another 10% will have a homosexual experience at some time. An even greater percentage of both sexes are bisexual, which, as Woody Allen pointed out, doubles the chance of a good night out on Saturdays. It also means that any pretending sexual Olympian is likely to have involvement in both directions – known as a well-travelled sexual compass. Or, at least, a very good story as to why not.

B

'A fast word about oral contraception. I asked a girl to go to bed with me, she said "no".'

Woody Allen

PREVENTING IT FROM WORKING

To assume a convincing air of responsibility and, heaven forbid, to avoid there being any possibility of being involved in the noisy and fund-depleting business which is actual procreation, understanding of contraception is all important. Once you are familiar with the workings, the next thing you need to know is how to stop them working.

From the moment men and women first realised that they actually enjoyed sex for the sake of sex, without any lasting consequences, they've been working on a way to prevent nature taking its course.

Contraceptive methods demonstrate *Homo sapiens* at his most outrageously inventive. Before the biotechnologically clever 'birth control pill' was invented, all contraceptives were based on putting something in the way of Mother Nature's intention. Placing something unpleasant between you and your partner was called 'barrier' contraception. Doing something unpleasant was called 'natural' contraception. We will deal with this latter form of practice first.

COITUS INTERRUPTUS

This is also known as the withdrawal method. It is almost impossible to practise with any degree of safety or certainty. Apart from the instinctive reluctance of most males to withdraw once they're where they really want to be, there is also the risk of premature ejaculation or, worse, something known as 'semen leakage'. This is a kind of sexual disorder sometimes found in men who have an over-vigorous masturbation habit. (Moral to sexually active women: try to avoid the type of dedicated wanker who insists on practising this particular method of contraception.)

As the comedian Billy Connolly said, 'I'd like to thank the withdrawal method, without which I wouldn't be here today.'

In the Bible, withdrawal was the method employed by Onan who 'spilt his seed on the ground' when pleasing himself with his sister-in-law. Unfortunately God was not impressed by his consideration and struck him dead. Let that be a lesson to all those who favour pulling out.

While a lethal smiting by an all-powerful deity might

be uncommon nowadays, an act of God may intervene in another way. Accidental pregnancy is estimated to occur at the rate of around 19% per year in regular withdrawers.

As the comedian Billy Connolly said, 'I'd like to thank the withdrawal method, without which I wouldn't be here today.'

RHYTHM METHOD ('FERTILITY AWARENESS')

The rhythm method involves collecting vaginal secretion and examining it to see if it has the consistency of egg white. Serious protagonists also use a hand-held computer to check their wee, or take their body temperature every day, and cease sexual activity when they heat up by a part of a degree. You might say that to label either of the above procedures 'natural' is a misuse of English, but so it goes.

With a failure rate of 23% a year, this method is not recommended for those who wish to stay childless.

THE SHEATH

We are led to believe that the contraceptive sheath was named after the Earl of Condom, court physician to King Charles II. The aim was to save His Majesty from the ravages of syphilis, and it was only when he was investigated for infertility that its contraceptive potential was recognised. The original sheaths were made from stretched sheep's intestines. Modern versions are moulded in transparently thin vulcanised rubber, or polyurethane, ribbed for sensitivity and available in more colours than a Ford Focus. They also come in various sizes for customer 'comfort'. Some sport strange nobbles for extra stimulation, though the extent to which this makes any difference at all is debatable.

The failure rate is 2% per year for careful couples; up to 15% for those with ragged fingernails.

The other advantage of the condom is, of course, its ability to help shield the couple from many, if by no means all, sexual diseases (*see* following chapter). You will entertain no argument against their use in casual sexual encounters. You might also add that you have yours custom-made.

THE DIAPHRAGM

Also known as 'the cap', this female rejoinder to the sheath originated in the Middle Ages when prostitutes in continental Europe started using half lemons as contraceptive devices. The threefold principle was that the juice acted as a spermicide, the inverted lemon wrapped itself around the cervix as a physical barrier and the citrus aroma was more attractive to the customer. We do not recommend this method as we imagine it would sting rather a lot. Oranges might be kinder. Pineapples are to be avoided.

The modern latex or silicone version, which must be used with spermicide and has a failure rate of between 6% and 39% per year, originates from late-19th-century Holland, hence the name Dutch cap. It is a tricky thing, and if inserted poorly can fly out like a small and ardour-dampening UFO.

THE SPONGE

To fathom the minds of the inventors of the condom and diaphragm is not too difficult a task. In trying to work out the mindset of the inventor of the contraceptive sponge, it is possible that we are dealing with a personality in crisis.

Popular in the USA, these disposable polyurethane pads are impregnated with a spermicidal cream which only works if it is lathered. The principle is that the woman wets the pad, works it into a foam and then inserts it to cover the cervix. So, if you know where your cervix is and can hit it first time with a slimy, soapy bodge of goo at a time when you probably have your mind on something rather more exciting, then this is the method for you. Not surprisingly, it is no longer the fashionable first choice.

SPERMICIDES

Users of barrier contraceptives who wish to improve safety standards will use a dash of cream, gel or foam.

The original materials used by South American Indians are said to have included pulped cactus, though it is not recorded whether the primary effect was by spermicidal action or spiking the invader. Macerated wolves' testes and oil-soaked wool were apparently popular ingredients in eastern Europe, and the ancient Egyptians are believed to have used pessaries made from a paste of honey and warm crocodile dung – though you could casually point out that it's likely any dung would do.

THE COIL (IUD)

No one is quite sure how intrauterine devices (IUDs) work or why the odd squiggly copper-lined plastic wires used nowadays are so effective as contraceptives. There are many millions of women walking around today with an alien object in their uterus and the majority of them are Chinese, which must mean something.

The Arabs have been 'protecting' their camels with stones for several thousand years. The dual principle is that a stone in the camel's cervix stops pregnancy and a couple of unfriendly rocks lower down blunts the ardour of any randy young buck camel trying the hump too often.

Some 2,500 years ago on the Greek island of Kos there is some evidence to suggest that Hippocrates used ivory, glass, ebony, platinum and diamond on his patients. Casanova carried a pouch of gold marbles with which, ultimately, to protect some of his ladies, hence confusing literary references to his golden balls (not the only thing he has in common with David Beckham).

The disadvantages of this method are that they can be painful to fit and sometimes get infected. The advantages are that they have a failure rate as low as 0.8–3% per year (designs vary) and that you can get on with the matter in hand without having to stop and grope for something else.

THE INTRAUTERINE SYSTEM (IUS)

Every modern woman's best friend, the internal device is worth its weight in diamonds. The IUS is a cross between the coil and the pill, releasing a small continuous dose of anti-baby hormones direct to the womb lining. It is as effective as female sterilisation, yet almost instantly reversible (provided you can find a friendly doctor who won't recoil from the procedure).

THE PILL

An estimated 20-billion-plus contraceptive pills are swallowed every year worldwide. If the Pope finally freed the Third World from perpetual fertility, then that number might double.

The most acceptable attitude to adopt when discussing 'the pill' is to highlight the moral dilemmas about fertility control, question the long-term effects on health, castigate male-dominated scientific medicine for the pill's essentially chauvinistic social role, and make very sure that either you or your partner is on it.

Modern pills contain minuscule amounts of hormones which are just enough to dupe the body into thinking it is slightly pregnant and so need not bother to produce eggs. The potential health-damaging effects of (unwanted) pregnancy are far greater than the pill-related risks implied in various research projects. A three-monthly injectable version sometimes assists the forgetful. Failure rates are as low as 0.1% per annum.

It was the Mexicans who found out centuries ago that Dioscorea, the wild yam vine, had both contraceptive and abortive properties. The first commercial versions of the pill were derived from the plant and were introduced in the USA in 1960, followed shortly afterwards by Australia, Germany and Britain. Not much progress has been made in the development of a male contraceptive pill, possibly because market research suggests a lack of interest among sexually active men (throughout the world) in taking it on a regular basis. A surprising number have, however, expressed interest in a 'male morning-after pill', which really makes you wonder how much some men understand about human procreation.

EMERGENCY CONTRACEPTION

Something you will do your damnedest to avoid, as all bluffers will be aware of the risks involved in unprotected sex. But, if you need to share your wisdom on the subject, you should be clear that there are two forms of emergency contraception. Like many a trapeze artist, the morning-after pill is more flexible than it sounds since it can be taken up to five days after unprotected sex (so it is actually the up-to-five-mornings-after pill), although it is most effective if started within 12 hours (and depending on the brand it might be necessary to take another 12 hours later). The morning-after pill is not foolproof but can reduce the risk of an unplanned pregnancy by up to 85%.

Alternatively, a copper-containing contraceptive coil can be fitted within five days of unprotected sex. This is 98% effective, but involves finding a fast-acting, knowledgable doctor within the timeframe, and with the correct equipment.

STERILISATION

In women the operation involves fastening a clip across

each fallopian tube via a tiny incision in the abdomen, or by using implants. In men the relevant tube is actually snipped by the surgeon (vasectomy). Some female operations can be reversed, but if you try to replumb the sterilised man it probably won't make a 'vas deferens'. (Very few people will get this reference, so point out that it's the bit that transports the sperm through the male reproductive system.)

In the 1970s doctors in New York devised a miniature gold and surgical-grade stainless steel three-way T-shaped tube known as the 'Bionyx Control Valve', which incorporated a tap which could be turned to the non-aligned position to obstruct the passage of sperm when needed. Unfortunately, invasive surgery was required every time the tap needed to be turned. Nothing has been seen or heard of it since.

ALTERNATIVE CONTRACEPTION

In ancient China, women were persuaded to drink 24 tadpoles in the spring to avoid pregnancy throughout the summer. If this failed then the following year they were advised to eat bees. The modern Chinese possess a substance called gossypol. Having established that men working in the cottonseed oil business were finding great difficulty in siring children, Chinese scientists isolated a chemical from the oil which guarantees to make any man subfertile. Unfortunately it also takes his ardour away and causes physical debilitation to a prepubescent state. US hormonal experts call it the 'Chinese takeaway'.

Ꞵ

'I have a friend who thinks he may have herpes,' says an anxious young man to his GP.

The doctor replies: 'Well, take him out and let's have a look at him.'

IT'S A BUG'S LIFE

The potential consequences of risky sexual activity are no laughing matter. The central point you should never forget when bluffing around this area is that – uniquely in this book – under no circumstances should you incriminate yourself by claiming to have first-hand experience.

Your game here is rather: to instruct, to sympathise, and to recall the poor chap whom you met that time in the Nigerian bush, whose hand you held after taking him to a field hospital and finding him a doctor to miraculously cure his syphilitically impaired sight.

The very least you should know is that an STI is a sexually transmitted infection, and STD a sexually transmitted disease. In truth, there is little difference between the two: the term STI was introduced as it sounded slightly less terrifying, and it was hoped people might be a bit braver about getting it treated and/or confessing to new partners that they had one. Bluffers should also know that it is possible to be infected (and to infect others) without necessarily having a disease.

Ancient diseases have Latin names to make them sound more respectable. Treponema pallidum (better known as syphilis, or 'pox'), Neisseria gonorrhoeae (clap), Pediculosis pubis (crabs) and Herpes genitalis (herpes) are just a few of the friends of the promiscuous or plain unlucky.

In the USA, an estimated 65-million-plus people are currently living with an incurable STI, and more than one in three of sexually active American youths will contract an STI by the age of 25. Public Health England figures show there were 420,000 cases of sexually transmitted infections diagnosed in 2017, with cases of syphilis continuing to rise.

These sort of alarming statistics are a very good argument for staying safely tucked up at home and merely cultivating the impression that you are a latter-day, uniquely gifted Casanova – rather than feeling the need actively to go out and try to become one.

However, the modern lover can, in most cases, overcome the problems of a nasty STI with a visit to the doctor and then to the prescriptions counter at the local pharmacy (actually probably not that local if you want to keep it quiet). But the best advice is to avoid contracting one in the first place. Note carefully: the three best ways of guarding against STIs can be described as follows: protection, protection and protection.

SYPHILIS

Pox is relatively rare nowadays. After an intensive public education campaign, the total number of reported cases in the UK dropped to less than 3,000 in 2011. Of these, only 313 occurred in women. About 60% of the male cases occurred in men who have had sex with men.

A big spot (chancre) on or near the fun bits below qualifies the bearer for membership of an elite victims' association boasting among its past members: Abraham, Bathsheba, Baudelaire, Al Capone, Catherine the Great, Cleopatra, Charlemagne, Columbus, Delius, Goya, Henry VIII, Herod (whose private parts were 'putrified and eaten by worms'), Julius Caesar, Keats, Mussolini, Napoleon, Samson (and Delilah), Schubert, Van Gogh and even good King Wenceslas (a detail oddly omitted by the carol).

The main drawback of syphilis is that if it is not treated, it waits around in the body for a decade or two, gradually causing blindness and heart disease, and often driving its owner-occupier insane before bringing about an unpleasant demise.

When it was rife in 16th-century Europe, the British called it the French disease, the French called it the Italian disease, the Italians called it the Spanish disease and the Spanish declared war on the British. When the Japanese introduced it to some of their conquered territories, they called it 'manka bassam' – the Portuguese disease. In this time of world harmony, it is now simply known as Old Joe.

NSU (NON-SPECIFIC URETHRITIS)

This affects as many as 100,000 people each year in Britain alone. Until recently it was also known as GOK (God only knows) since the bugs which caused it were not identified. It turns out that the offending organism is usually that called Chlamydia trachomatis, an unholy microbe which, like other bacteria, can be killed by the right drugs but, like a virus, is not always identifiable under a light microscope.

The bad news is that it can go for months without making itself known and can, in the meantime, render you infertile (sometimes forever). The good news is that it is relatively easily treated with antibiotics.

Q: What's green and eats nuts?
A: Gonorrhoea.

GONORRHOEA

The 'perilous infirmity of burning' was recorded as early as the 12th century in London brothels. The French preferred the term *la pisse chaude*. It claims more than 20,000 new victims each year in the UK. Until recently, the merest whiff of penicillin was enough to make the bugs commit mass suicide, but most modern gonococci are made of sterner stuff.

HERPES

Genital herpes is caused by the same viruses as cold sores on the lips; bluffers might therefore point out that the fashion for oral sex is responsible for the current popularity of this infection, which acquires around

30,000 new victims each year, over 18,000 of whom are women – and affirm that it is less easily shared when the sores are not visible.

If you catch herpes, the chances are that you now have a friend for life. All is not gloom and despondency though. Like any good friend, herpes only shows up occasionally, usually at inconvenient moments and with decreasing frequency as you get older.

TRICHOMONAS VAGINALIS

A microscopic parasite which is said to naturally inhabit the vagina without any obvious symptoms. However, if it starts breeding copiously, it develops into an infection which can be passed on to others by – guess what sort of activity. Of all the varieties of sexually transmitted disease it is the only one which can definitely/probably/possibly (depending on who you talk to) be caught from the seat of a lavatory.

CONDYLOMATA

The fancy name for genital warts. You will, of course, have no personal experience of these unwelcome visitors. But you might need to pronounce on them nonetheless.

They are caused by viruses and can be passed on through intimate sexual contact. So if you see anything resembling one on your or a partner's reproductive organs (or anywhere near them, especially if it's 'mucosal') you really need to seek treatment as soon as possible. Forget anything you've heard about alternative medicine remedies or extracts of mandrake root, warts need to be zapped with maximum force and without mercy.

If you need to communicate to unwanted guests at a boring dinner party that it is time for them to go, a bluffer would do well to render a description of the most evil and ugliest of genital warts from any good medical textbook. Look under Buschke-Löwenstein Giant Condylomata, preferably not on a full stomach.

Q: What's worse than lobsters
on your piano?
A: Crabs on your organ...

CRABS

If the aforementioned diseases represent the flora of the nether regions then Pediculosis pubis is the fauna. But wee jumping creatures in the genital hedgerow should not be made the subject of a conservation order. Happily, treating these pubic crustaceans is usually as simple as shaving the area, and then using topical cream to (attempt) to cure the itch.

AIDS

AIDS is not yet curable and is spread by HIV, a virus with more disguises than Jim Carrey but less subtle in its lethality. Anyone who has ever had sex with another person can theoretically be a carrier. High-risk groups include promiscuous gay men, injecting drug users, and those who are from countries with a high AIDS rate, such as regions in central and southern Africa.

Sigmund Freud was a great smoker. This may or may not have been related to his belief that tobacco is a substitute for masturbation.

LET'S TALK ABOUT SEXOLOGY

All bluffers should have some degree of familiarity with the psychology of sex. It conveys expertise and understanding like few other aspects of the game. An in-depth knowledge of what motivates us to surrender to one of the most powerful human instincts suggests that you might actually have a reasonable idea about how to do it.

Here are the key players you need to be familiar with.

RICHARD FREIHERR VON KRAFFT-EBING

In the late 1800s the German psychiatrist Krafft-Ebing published *Psychopathia Sexualis* – a landmark text of sexual mania and deviation, which established sexology as a scientific discipline. A man of his time, he suggested that 'perversions' (i.e., any sexual activity which did not lead to procreation), such as homosexuality, were caused by degeneracy, often as a result of a weak genetic line.

In the seminal work, he described four categories of what he called 'cerebral neuroses': paradoxia (sexual desire at the wrong time of life), anaesthesia (insufficient sexual desire at any time of life), hyperaesthesia (excessive sexual desire at every time of life) and paraesthesia (misdirected sexual desire involving one or more perversions, usually but not always involving life). The only neurosis likely to be of interest to the average bluffer is number three, but it is as well to know of the others (if only to ensure that you don't confuse them).

You could also expound on the more entertaining oddities with which he categorised various kinds of perversions, as well as some of the terms he was responsible for bringing into general circulation:

Sadism A sexual delight in inflicting pain. Though the practice was already recognised by psychiatry, Krafft-Ebing coined the term 'sadism', basing it on the brutal depravity delineated in the novels of the Marquis de Sade.

Masochism A sexual delight in receiving pain. Krafft-Ebing derived this term from the name of the contemporary author Leopold von Sacher-Masoch, who signed up to be a slave to his mistress Baroness Fanny Pistor (yes, really), begging her to wear fur as often as possible, especially when she was feeling particularly cruel, and wrote a novella heavily based on their adventures, *Venus in Furs*.

Depending on your audience, it may be worth concluding your references to Krafft-Ebing with:

- a respectful nod to his forward-looking realisation that homosexual activity should be decriminalised, because it was an inclination that the patient couldn't control; and

- a disappointed sigh that he perceived women as sexually entirely passive.

HAVELOCK ELLIS

Next to Krafft-Ebing, British doctor and psychologist Havelock Ellis is the other granddaddy of modern sexology. He is notable for challenging the sexual repression of the Victorian age. A social reformer, as well as a founding member of the Fabian Society, Ellis believed in free love, the emancipation of women, sexual equality and birth control. It is fair to say that he was somewhat ahead of his time.

When holding forth, a key text to which you might allude is his *Studies in the Psychology of Sex* – a remarkable six-volume work published in 1897, which was the first medical textbook to attempt a sensible understanding of homosexuality. Like Krafft-Ebing, he was a pioneer in not regarding homosexual activity as a crime, but treating it as a recurrent part of human sexuality. In the outcry that naturally followed the book's publication, George Bernard Shaw and Bertrand Russell were among those who leapt to its defence.

Potential students should be warned, however, that as well as being innovative, thought-provoking and decades ahead of its time, *Studies* is monumentally dull. You are not advised to read it in bed unless you have difficulty sleeping.

Ellis also developed the concepts of auto-eroticism and narcissism (both of which were taken up by Freud, *see* below).

You can season your anecdotes about Ellis with some fascinating facts about his life. One of the leading authorities of his era in terms of sexual enlightenment, at 32, and still a virgin, he married a lesbian and while she had numerous female lovers it would appear they never consummated their union. Furthermore, he suffered impotence which he could only really overcome when he had the opportunity to watch a woman urinate. Whatever turns you on…

The last, more unfortunate detail, is that Ellis was a supporter of the then fashionable (pre-Nazi) idea of eugenics.

SIGMUND FREUD

Sigismund Schlomo Freud is the great Austrian neurologist who has enriched our language, and the bluffer's lexicon, with his theories. The essential point you'll want to hark on about is Freud's belief that sexual desire is the primary motivation for mankind. Somewhere along the line he also invented psychoanalysis.

Latterly, and noisily, Freud has been denounced as not terribly scientific and rather sexist. None of this matters. You will need to be aware of the fundamental tenets of his work so that you can look suitably appalled should anyone be ignorant enough to confess that they don't know what you are talking about.

Free association By around 1896, Freud abandoned hypnosis in his treatment of neurotics in favour of free association – in which his patients would talk about whatever occurred to them. This frequently involved sexual fantasy.

Oedipus complex An idea first referenced in *The Interpretation of Dreams* (1899) in which he argues that dreams are manifestations of repressed sexual desire. 'Oedipus complex' refers to the emotions of a boy who wishes to kill his father and sleep with his mother. Hamlet had a similar problem.

Id Conscious (impulsive and childlike, operating on the pleasure principle).

Ego Unconscious (organised, realistic).

Super-ego Preconscious (critical and moralising).

To be honest, these elements of the consciousness are easily confused; best really to litter them knowingly without any attempt at understanding which is which. Like everyone else does.

Life drive The erotic, libidinous part of yourself. (This will be strong, naturally.)

Death drive The aggressive parts of you which crave annihilation. (This will be weak, naturally.)

Make up as much as you want about these drives; nobody really understands what Freud was on about. Just don't claim that he invented the hard drive. That came a century or so later.

On a more personal note, it's possible that Freud slept with his sister-in-law after the death of her fiancé (and that she even aborted his child). He was an early user and proponent of cocaine as a stimulant and antidepressant. He was also a great smoker. This may or may not have been related to his belief that tobacco is a substitute for masturbation.

ALFRED KINSEY

In 1938, Dr Alfred C Kinsey, a Harvard-trained professor of zoology, was asked to coordinate a marriage course at Indiana University. Unable to answer his students' questions on the subject of sex, he set out to create the largest sexual survey ever done. His findings, you will say, shocked Middle America (not to mention Middle England).

For the first part of his career, Kinsey's passion was the gall wasp. He collected three million of the things and produced the definitive work on subspecies in the gall wasp world. Applying the same method to the examination of several thousand sexual histories, he interviewed some 18,000 people (or so he claimed). In 1948 he published *Sexual Behavior in the Human Male* –

soon followed by a similar – and similarly revolutionary – insight into female sexuality.

Some of Kinsey's findings which you may wish to have at your fingertips include:

- Some 37% of white males had reached orgasm through homosexual contact.

- 4% of men and 2% of women are exclusively homosexual and up to 6% of men are homosexual for a significant part of their adolescence.

- 98% of men and over 50% of women masturbate.

- One wife in four had committed adultery.

- Women could have multiple orgasms.

Adopting a suitably professorial air, you might want to ask your audience to imagine the world which Kinsey inhabited. America was God-fearing – and Kinsey's Methodist father especially so. When he began teaching at Indiana, the university's president still came to work in a horse and cart. Many Americans disputed evolution. Moreover, there was a strong McCarthyite crackdown on homosexuality (when the alcoholic, homophobic, demagogic old fraud wasn't cracking down on imagined communists).

As well as being brave, however, Kinsey may have been a bit slapdash. As your listeners digest some of the statistics he uncovered, you might interject a note or two of caution about his methodology – especially an alleged tendency to present material from one respondent as coming from several. But that's market research for you.

Notably, in 1956 Kinsey was detained by US Customs for carrying pornography, which he claimed to be essential for his work. He was also known to hang out in the Astor Bar, a famous gay pick-up joint in New York, but this cannot be taken as proof that he was himself gay. His friend Gore Vidal explained: 'I like to think that it was by observing the easy trafficking at the Astor that he figured out what was obvious to most of us, though as yet undreamed of by American society at large: perfectly "normal" young men, placed outside the usual round of family and work, will run riot with each other…Kinsey gave me a copy of *Sexual Behavior in the Human Male,* with an inscription, complimenting me on my "work in the field". Thanks, Doc. But it wasn't *all* work.'

MASTERS AND JOHNSON

The Reproductive Biology Research Project is the name of the work carried out by William Masters and Virginia Johnson at the Washington University in St Louis. The most famous book they produced from it was *Human Sexual Response,* which saw the light of day in April 1966.

Between 1957 and 1965 they watched what happens when a sexually mature man or woman enjoys sex. Some 382 anonymous women and 312 anonymous men masturbated or had sexual intercourse a total of 10,000 times under laboratory conditions, i.e., in front of a team of wholly disinterested professionals. Insofar as anyone choosing to get laid in a laboratory is 'normal', these measurements have for over 20 years defined the averages and the outer limits of normal sexual experience.

Discoveries include the fact that men ejaculate between three and seven times during orgasm at an average rate of 1.25 times per second and that women can have up to 12 contractions during orgasm with some able to manage an instant repeat. The record was 25 contractions in 43 seconds. The clitoris is back in position within 10 seconds of completing an orgasm, the vagina returns to its normal state within 15 minutes but the cervix remains gaping for slightly longer.

'Perfectly "normal" young men, placed outside the usual round of family and work, will run riot with each other.'

Many of their findings were the result of a novel technique in which a see-through imitation penis, individually tailored to the requirements of the female participant, was inserted into her Jade Room and manipulated in realistically rhythmic fashion. This enabled cameras and fibrescopes to see and measure exactly what was happening.

No doubt their shared experiences contributed to the fact that Ms Johnson later became Mrs Masters.

THE HITE REPORT

Shere Hite may sound like a penis enlargement cream, or an anagram of something rather more scatological, but she is the American-born German sex educator and journalist who achieved fame and fortune by interviewing women (who answered a magazine advertisement) about their sex lives. The Hite Report was a sort of vox pop Kinsey with a *Cosmopolitan* bias, published in the mid-1970s. If you hear someone stating with confidence that 39% of all women under 35 feature Barry Manilow's nose in their masturbatory fantasies, then the information might well have come from Hite.

It is worth knowing that in 1981 Ms Hite did a similar study on men. Barry Manilow's nose did not feature significantly in their masturbatory fantasies.

HEROIC LOVERS

The accolade of 'great lover' is attributed to very few. It is important to be familiar with the stories of some of these adept practitioners, but caution is advised. When relating their exploits you should temper each one with a healthy measure of disbelief. The following selection consists of some of the more reliable accounts.

KING DAVID AND KING SOLOMON

The Old Testament translators used some splendid euphemisms when speaking of sex. To 'lie with' and to 'know' may be translated into modern vernacular as to 'have' and to 'give one to'.

King David had eight wives and ten concubines. Only when well past pensionable age did he suffer a sudden loss of power as his loins 'gat no heat'. The elders sent for a virgin, called Abishag (quite seriously). Alas, even she could not stoke his fire and he died soon after.

King Solomon specialised in dowries. By the time of his death he is said to have had 700 wives in addition to his 300 concubines, many of them acquired from around the known world, including Egypt, his favourite being the Queen of Sheba. You might care to suggest, should anyone ask what made her so special, that she was the only one whose name he could remember.

CHOU HSIN AND YANG TI

Chou Hsin was a Chinese playboy king of the Shang Dynasty, who lived around 1500 BC. He was said to have regularly entertained ten partners in one session and to have invented his own 'position', involving strutting around the room with an impaled woman entwined around his waist. Unfortunately the authenticity of this tale is not lent further conviction by the additional 'facts', namely that he was nearly 2.5 metres tall and could kill tigers and leopards with his bare hands.

More likely are the accounts of the behaviour of his compatriot Yang Ti, emperor of the Sui Dynasty in the seventh century AD. He had one queen, two deputy queens, six official consorts, 72 royal occasionals and a palace staff of 3,000 handmaidens. Bluffers might be particularly interested in his idea of a good picnic. If ever he went journeying around his empire, he ensured that among the caravan were ten carts, each accommodating a naked maiden draped on a red satin sheet like a prawn on a smoked salmon canapé.

MESSALINA

Valeria Messalina was the wife of the Roman emperor Claudius. She married him when she was 16 but was already an established man-eater. A typical story of her antics stemmed from a time when Claudius was away on business. She was left both miffed and unsated, so challenged a well-known Roman whore to a 'man contest'. Messalina won by servicing as many as 50 prominent Roman citizens. She died at 30, probably of old age.

CLEOPATRA

Apart from bathing in asses' milk and hailing a variety of Caesars, Queen Cleopatra's greatest claim to fame was as the ancient world's finest fellatrix. She was reported once to have performed her art on 100 Roman soldiers in one evening, from which one can surmise that she was a sucker for any man in uniform. Her name in Greek is Merichane which is held to mean 'she who gapes wide for ten thousand'.

GENGHIS KHAN

When he wasn't gleefully eviscerating and mutilating his many enemies (and some of his friends) the ruthless Mongolian hegemonist was also on a personal crusade to impregnate as many women as time permitted during the remarkable speed of his empire building (stretching from the Pacific to eastern Europe). Such was his fondness for the intimate company of fertile females that he left a vast genetic legacy with some estimates putting his personal dynasty at around 16 million male descendants alive today. This is a useful factoid for bluffers to quote, because the 'research' was carried out by 'Russian scientists', and it is impossible to prove or disprove. It is enough to say with confidence that sex was as much a tool of power as a right of conquest for the Great Khan and he applied himself to it enthusiastically. In the process he sired a staggering number of little Genghises.

CASANOVA

The most famous of the great lovers was born in Venice in 1725. His name was Giacomo Casanova (Jack Newhouse in English) and, according to a contemporary, 'He would be a good-looking man if he were not ugly.' He is notorious as much for the sheer number of his sexual conquests (and the fact that they included five sisters and their mother, a hunchback with 'an excitingly misplaced vulva', and two unrepentant nuns) as the joy with which he recorded them in his memoirs. You should know that he was actually something of a scholar who hung out with Voltaire, Mozart and Goethe.

Casanova started young, being expelled from a seminary at the age of 16 for immoral conduct. His style was that of a collector. For him a woman's most attractive feature was not her virtue but her cooperation in his essentially selfish quest to try sex in all its forms. The acts he remembered were those with the youngest, oldest, tallest, shortest, fattest, most disfigured and most disturbed of his sexual partners. He could recall details like the number of chairs employed in the performance, the public park involved, and the position of the lady's left foot at the moment of orgasm. It was the faces and surnames which eluded him.

LORD BYRON

George Gordon, better known as Lord Byron (his title was inherited from a great uncle), was the most celebrated poet of the Romantic period during the early 19th century. He earns his place in this chapter for his achievement in ensuring that his name became synonymous with the language of love and passion. Byron had a voracious sexual appetite, once writing to his publisher that he had slept with over 200 women while he lived briefly in Venice in his late 20s. Women were said to swoon at the sight of him and his reputation as an expert lover (largely self-promoted) certainly did his endless quest for intimate female company no harm (although most biographers agree that he wasn't too fussy about the gender of his sexual partners.) As the darling of London literary society, he was adored by aristocratic women of the time – drawn to him by his sensual good looks and bosom-heaving poetry. The epithet 'mad, bad and dangerous to know' was coined by the novelist and socialite Lady Caroline Lamb to describe the young poet, characteristics which clearly served only to make him even more attractive to her – evinced by a short-lived but passionate affair in 1812. After Byron ended their relationship Lamb tried to stab herself and then sent Byron a snippet of her pubic hair, a particularly thoughtful gesture which he is understood to have declined.

RASPUTIN

That the Russian 'mystic' was an unscrupulous charlatan is not in doubt. Having inveigled his way into the court of

Tsar Nicholas II as a 'holy man' who correctly predicted that the Tsarina would deliver a male heir within a year, Rasputin set about entrenching his position by claiming to be 'a Christ in miniature' and swiftly developing a religious cult around himself. In fact he was an illiterate Siberian peasant who considered the serial seduction of women to be some kind of spiritual duty. After a short stay in a monastery in his late 20s, he claimed that by sleeping with women he could take on their sins and thus help them find the 'grace of God'. 'I don't degrade you, I purify you,' he would assure his female followers before 'rejoicing' with each of them. These energetic bouts of rejoicing were unlikely to be a pleasant experience for the women in question. Rasputin had apparently terrible personal hygiene, rotting stumps for teeth and appalling breath. After one final night of debauchery, which involved copious quantities of Madeira and the company of some of his most devoted followers, he was lured into a trap believing that a tryst had been arranged with a beautiful young courtier with whom he had long yearned to rejoice. In fact he was plied with cyanide which failed to kill him, and then shot – which also failed to kill him, and finally bludgeoned to death before being thrown into a nearby river.

ERROL FLYNN

Hollywood's most libidinous swordsman, who inspired the saying 'In like Flynn', had few rivals for his crown. He was described by one biographer as 'probably the greatest symbol of masculinity and virility developed in the modern age'. In the words of another writer, Flynn had 'a quite staggering appetite for sex', but the Tasmanian-born actor himself claimed to be perplexed by his reputation. In his autobiography published after his death in Vancouver in 1959, he wrote innocently: 'I made about forty five pictures, but what had I become? I knew all too well: a phallic symbol. All around the world I was, as a name and personality, equated with sex'. In truth his widely publicised sexual profligacy did the talking, and he clearly revelled in his role as the world's most famous womaniser. One of his co-stars recalled going to Flynn's dressing room and seeing the star naked and grinning in his armchair, with one woman on top of him and another waiting her turn. Bluffers might be interested in putting one particular urban myth regarding Flynn's legendary appendage to rest. According to the Vancouver coroner, writing some time after Flynn's death from a heart attack at 50, '[He] was no larger and no smaller in his stature, his jewels, his endowment, than any other man. So there may well be hope for the inferior feeling males of the world if, indeed, that's the sort of thing they're concerned about.'

The male sex bluffer, of course, has no reason to be concerned about anything of the sort.

JOHN F KENNEDY

No intern or secretary, or even nubile visitor, was said to be entirely sure of protecting her virtue while 'Jack'

Kennedy occupied the White House in the early 1960s. The charismatic young President's reputation as a serial womaniser is supported by contemporary accounts and also by his own alleged admission that he felt physically ill if he didn't have regular sex with partners other than his long-suffering wife. Apparently there was no shortage of patriotic admirers willing to assist him in this respect.

When he wasn't having private audiences with star struck young women, the 35th President of the United States is also said to have worked his way through a veritable cast list of leading actresses including, famously, Marilyn Monroe. And if you believe everything you read, Marlene Dietrich, nearly 20 years his senior, was also on his list of lovers.

In attempting to understand his reportedly insatiable sexual appetite, and what bluffers will know that many others don't, is that Kennedy's heroic philandering may have been the result of the medication he was taking for Addison's Disease, a disorder affecting the immune system. Bluffers can state knowledgeably that one of the side-effects of the powerful drugs he was prescribed could have been an uncontrollable increase in his sex drive. During a 1961 meeting in Bermuda with the patrician British Prime Minister Harold Macmillan, Kennedy is reported to have observed, 'I wonder how it is with you, Harold? If I don't have a woman for three days, I get terrible headaches.' Macmillan's response is not known.

SEXUAL HISTORY

Many modern commentators have been known to contend that people today live in immoral (or if you prefer, 'liberated') times. This quaint idea fails to withstand close examination. There is endless conversational mileage to be derived from the position you might consider taking that, compared with other successful civilisations of years gone by, contemporary society is sexually sensitive to the point of prudery.

Admittedly, sexual historians have their work cut out sifting the facts from a wealth of nice ideas. Most recorded information from past centuries dwells on matters of little consequence such as politics, imperial human-interest stories, invasions, massacres and that sort of thing. It is rare to find items relating to immediate concerns like food, booze, sex or folk singing. To add to these difficulties, many of the accounts which do exist are hopelessly prejudiced, either due to censorship or lecherous exaggeration. None of this, of course, should in any way impede your using them to full effect. The history of sex furnishes you with bluffing gold.

EARLY MAN

Among the rock paintings in the Sahara (dating from 4000–5000 BC) are several depicting early man rutting with early woman. Dirty doodling is perhaps the oldest art form on Earth, a tradition which continues on the back of doors in public conveniences.

Prehistoric humans also had a taste for dildos. If you ever find yourself needing to defend the use of sex toys, you could point out that we have been entertaining ourselves with them for as long as we have been able to fashion tools: a double-ended baton from the Gorge d'Enfer region in France dating to the Upper Palaeolithic era (more than 10000 BC), features two carved phalluses set at the same angle designed, presumably, to satisfy two women at the same time.

THE EGYPTIANS

The Egyptians invented pyramids, mummies, pageboy haircuts and eye make-up. Lesser known but infinitely more useful creations included writing paper. The earliest known forerunners of the 'blue' media were a collection of porno hieroglyphics and 'adult-only' papyruses found in the Nile Valley. A comparison with the blue movie output of Copenhagen's Color Climax Corporation will show that while the technology has improved, the plot remains essentially the same.

The Egyptians' other claim to fame was that their royal household survived for many hundreds of years on the principle of keeping it, i.e., sex, in the family.

European royalty has a tradition of marrying distant cousins but the Egyptians were more choosy. In order of preference the ideal child-bearer for the son of an Egyptian king was:

- his mother;
- his sister; or
- his daughter.

Which gives a whole new meaning to family affairs.

THE CHINESE

The ancient Chinese produced a greater variety of erotic *objets d'art* in the first millennium BC than arguably any civilisation before or since. Pottery vases, statuettes, jewellery, engraved elephant tusks and even coins of the realm exist from that period, showing men and women fornicating in every conceivable position with each other, beasts of the field and even themselves.

The Taoists claimed at one point that immortality could be achieved by those who excelled between the sheets. This led to the imperial court calling up legions of beautiful handmaidens to assist the emperor in his quest. It also led to Taoism gaining the approval of the court. A few years later, we are assured that they suggested that young men could rise to a higher spiritual plane if they sought a deep and meaningful friendship with a heifer. Presumably, the inscrutable logic behind this was that by then there were too few handmaidens to go round.

THE GREEKS

In a society free from the moral majority, the Athenians held that sexuality was a gift from the Gods and should be indulged as freely and widely as felt natural.

Brothels had been known around the eastern Mediterranean since 2000BC, but the Athenians were the first to bring them under state control. The aim was to quell rowdiness and the spread of disease. The Athens exchequer cleaned up the brothels too – for the first and last time in history, sex was subject to a purchase tax.

The Greeks also brought homosexuality out of the closet. An ever-practical people, they realised that a certain proportion of their population preferred partners of their own sex – and that locking them away in all-male prisons was unlikely to persuade them otherwise.

THE ROMANS

During the heyday of their empire, the Romans had a reputation for civilised behaviour and strict-ish moral codes. But with its decline and fall, a series of ineffectual and patently unhinged emperors gave licence to ever more extreme forms of pleasure-seeking while maintaining impossibly strict legislation on the behaviour of the plebs.

Tiberius, perhaps the least hinged of the lot, being aware that it was illegal to put a virgin to death, decreed that executioners rape their victims in public view prior to the killing. He was described by the official historian of the time as 'a filthy old man'.

Nero preferred larger-scale spectacles. He was the Cecil B DeMille of orgiastic sex. A great believer in audience participation, his creations blurred the boundaries between eroticism, violence and chaos, in a way that was not repeated until 1,800 years later, by Sigmund Freud.

Nero was raised by a barber and a male ballet dancer. Perhaps if he had been in analysis, the history of the Western world would have been very different.

THE EARLY CHRISTIANS

Christians were the first folk in western Europe to bring a pandemic niceness to the way they treated each other. Their idea of antisocial behaviour was to carve fishes on the wall – and let's face it, there is nothing less erotic than a fish.

The New Testament laid down a moral code which recommended monogamous marriage and fidelity. This was a sensible way of limiting sexually transmitted disease and single-parent families in the days before condoms, penicillin and the Department of Health and Social Security.

Early Christians permitted premarital sex, provided it was with a view to checking out a prospective partner and not merely a means of scattering one's seed. Equally, they saw homosexuality as a bit of a waste of energy rather than a mortal sin. Misogyny, frigidity and hypocrisy were products of a later era – the Holy Roman Empire – when the Christian uprising had turned into just another revolting revolt.

St Augustine, a theologian from Roman Africa who was born in 354 at the end of the early Christian era, provided some of the better lines in all of the commentary on Christianity and sex. Hedonistic as a youth and apparently obsessed with sex in The City of God, he discussed how 'At times, without intention, the body stirs on its own, insistent…at other times, it leaves a straining lover in the lurch.' However, his best, and most famous utterance is surely: 'Grant me chastity and continence. But not yet.'

THE CONTINENTALS

Religion, power and sex have always been intertwined. The early popes tended to prefer the last two.

John XII was asked to leave for turning the St John Lateran into a bordello. Leo VIII's departure was less public – he is said to have had a stroke while engaged in the act. Alexander VI got caught out for holding a super binge at tithe-payers' expense when he invited the prostitutes of Rome to come and dance naked in front of the papal court. Unfortunately things got out of hand and he ended up offering prizes to the men who, in the audience's opinion, had pleasured the most girls. This rumoured propensity for hosting wild orgies must be balanced against his patronage of the arts (if not, perhaps, reports that he fathered his own daughter's child).

All these shenanigans were several hundred years before the Medicis and Borgias, whose specialities were incest, perversion of youth and the odd piece of gratuitous violence. Balthasar Cossa, the man who was recruited as candidate to heal the Great Schism which once promised to eradicate Catholicism, was a breath of fresh air in comparison. His memoirs revealed only the faintest smattering of close relatives, married women and Holy Sisters among his many conquests.

In France, scions of the Louis dynasty were hardly bastions of propriety. Louis XIII married at 14 when he may well have been prepubescent. The poor lad was made to consummate the marriage the same night. It was some time before he could attempt a repeat performance. Louis XIV, in addition to siring 14 heirs, formed a bevy of mistresses. He paid the better ones by granting them the income from a tobacco and meat tax imposed on the citizens of Paris. In later life he developed an anal fistula which made sex so painful that he turned to religion and château-building instead.

Louis XV's sexual appetite was notorious, and he commissioned the building of a different kind of château – the Parc aux Cerfs, a mansion in the grounds of Versailles where several dozen young *femmes* were installed for his pleasure at considerable cost to the public purse. The French Revolution took place shortly after his death.

THE BRITISH

In Britain, neither the ancient nor Holy Roman influence is easily discerned. Early attitudes to sex were shaped more by the Vikings and other bands of hoodlums. Virginity was retained by the faster runners.

The Anglo-Saxon language had no word for adultery and Dark Age Britain wasn't known for its morality. Chaucer's *The Canterbury Tales* will attest that coupling with friends and acquaintances was seen as fair sport. It is from this era that the natives inherited most of the monosyllabic grunts which pass for profanities in modern English.

The Normans brought them the *droit de seigneur* – the custom by which the virgins of the parish were allowed the privilege on the eve of their wedding to be deflowered by the lord of the manor. Feudal lords were also entitled to claim unpaid tithes from villeins (feudal tenants) in the form of sexual favours from the womenfolk. One account exists of an abbot inheriting *le droit*.

James I (and VI of Scotland) was the original gay cavalier – the first monarch to flaunt his sexual preferences.

Surprisingly little is known about the sexual practices of the Middle Ages. The success of a good Catholic policy of monogamy and fidelity can be gauged by the fact that there was an epidemic of syphilis in the late 1400s which had the experts predicting an eradication of the race within 20 years.

It is unlikely that such concerns altered the national attitude to promiscuity, however. James I (and VI of Scotland) was the original gay cavalier – the first monarch to flaunt his sexual preferences. He referred to boyfriend George Villiers, 25 years his junior, as 'sweet child and wife' before making him Duke of Buckingham and agreeing to immortalise his name in an area off the Strand in London – these include: George Court, Villiers Street, Duke Street, Buckingham Street and several back alleys.

Samuel Pepys and other authors of the 1600s describe whoring as commonplace – just one of the options for an otherwise dull Thursday night. King Charles II indulged openly with Nell Gwyn and enough others to sire 17 illegitimate children – a fine testimony to the Earl of Condom's efforts. Fertility was not a problem in the 1600s if Mary Honeywood of Lenham, Kent, is anything to go by. Her tombstone claims that she was survived by 16 children, 114 grandchildren, 228 great-grandchildren and 9 great-great-grandchildren. This feat still stands as a British record, nearly 400 years after her death.

In the next century, Queen Anne had 18 pregnancies, which might account for the shape of her legs*.

THE VICTORIANS

The vast majority of modern sexual hang-ups can be blamed on the Victorians. They were not pillars of moral rectitude. They were simply confused. The idea that copulation was strictly for populating, that a lady performs sex as a duty not a pleasure, that masturbation

---

* Furniture made in the reign of Queen Anne has legs described as 'cabriole', i.e., convex in the upper part and concave in the lower.

leads to blindness and insanity, that unrepentant fornicators would suffer the flames of eternal damnation and that piano legs were indecent and should be covered up, are all the products of Victorian minds.

Ironically it was during the Victorian era that sadomasochism was first recognised as a sexual activity. The late 1800s saw the heyday in London of brothels specialising in the procurement of children and the employment of corseted whip-wenches catering for flagellation and bondage. The position of mistress almost became an acceptable role in polite society and at the commercial end of the same spectrum the brothel-keeper was elevated to the post of Madame. In better circles, she often made as great a fortune as her wealthier clients.

THE MODERN ERA

Look around. The classified advertisements for sex chat lines in top shelf magazines are undiminished by the plethora of live sex webcam sites, the staggering number of escort/prostitution listing websites, the burgeoning popularity of sex-finding apps, and the sheer volume of freely accessible pornographic material on the internet.* It is clear to see that the more things change, the more they stay the same.

---

*The popular urban myth that the online sex industry has larger revenues than Microsoft, Google, Amazon, eBay, Yahoo and Apple combined, maybe isn't so far-fetched after all.

There's no point in pretending that you know everything about sex – nobody does – but if you've got this far and you've absorbed at least a modicum of the information and advice contained within these pages, then you will almost certainly know more than 99% of the rest of the human race about what sex is, why it is so profoundly enjoyable and rewarding, and how you can pretend to be better at it than you are.

What you now do with this information is up to you, but here's a suggestion: be confident about your new-found knowledge, see how far it takes you, but, above all, have fun using it. You are now a bona fide expert in the art of bluffing about the world's most pleasurable pastime. And two final words of advice: be safe.

GLOSSARY

Algolagnia Clinical term for sado-masochism, the 'pleasures' derived from giving or receiving pain.

Auto-eroticism The ability to contort the body in such a way as to have oral sex with oneself. As simulated by bisexual dancer Nijinsky.

Balls deep A crude description for deep penetrative sexual intercourse.

Banjo string Medically known as the frenulum (translation: 'little bridle'), this is the fine length of skin on the underside of the penis linking the helmet to the foreskin and main shaft. Generally attention is paid most to it a) in proficient fellatio and b) in not-very-proficient sex, where over-zealous efforts can cause it to snap – a painful and often bloody occurrence.

Bestiality Sexual activity with other species. It is illegal; for it to be otherwise would be a gross abuse of animal rights. You should stick to eating them instead.

Bondage Self-explanatory. In a sexual context it involves varying degrees of restraint involving perfectly normal practices such as submission, slavery, occasional humiliation, and a detailed knowledge of knots.

Bonk Exclusively British word for the act of having sex, along with **Shag** (offensive), **Screw** (even more offensive) and **Nookie** (relatively harmless).

Brewer's droop Erectile failure when caught on the hop.

Bungle in the jungle The opposite of a 'shaven haven'. Also, the act of exploring a 'lady garden' or 'front bottom'. Take your pick.

Catamite A sodomite with twin hulls.

Condomplate To contemplate the use of a condom.

Contraceptives Drugs or devices designed for use on every conceivable occasion.

Cowgirl Position adopted in the act of coitus where the female sits astride her partner, facing him/her in order to simulate the act of riding a horse. Saddles, bits, spurs, chaps and carrots are optional accessories.

Cybersex Using the internet in order to make onanism (see below) more interesting.

Detumescence Technical term for the droop.

Dildo A penis substitute, usually more impressive than the original.

Dogging Observing or participating in exhibitionist sexual activity in a public place, generally a car, using the feeble excuse of taking the dog for a walk.

Doughnut bumper Irreverent description of a female person who engages in the Sapphic arts.

Duvet A quilt complex.

Eonism The alternative name for transvestitism. (An anagram of Simeon or Simone.)

Eros Greek god of love. His Roman equivalent was Cupid.

Erotic act Cupid stunt.

Erotic art Pornography with silk underpants.

Erotic body part Cunning stunt.

Exhibitionism A display of erotic art.

Fetishism The use of a talisman to achieve sexual arousal. The fetishist can become obsessed by a particular part of the body, a type of clothing or some other inanimate object. Obsessions with rubberwear are often seen as kinky, unless involved in scuba-diving.

Fornication Sexual activity between unmarried people.

Frottage A covert means of achieving sexual enjoyment by rubbing up against a member of the opposite sex in a crowded place, such as a tube train or the checkout at Tesco. Also known, wrongly, as frotteurism.

Gay Homosexual, whether male or female, happy or miserable. Originally a 19th-century term for prostitute (of both sexes).

Gay bars What Oscar Wilde sat behind in Reading Gaol.

Gigolo Italian folk hero. Part jiggle. Part low.

Gokuraku ojo A kind of sexual hara-kiri involving the belief that it is possible to be rogered to death and that, if you have to go, it's as good a way as any.

Gomorrah Where the Sodomites went to give their bottoms a rest. Nothing to do with gonorrhoea, although on the other hand…

Gooseberry bush Where babies came from before sex was invented.

Guilt When what you know to be nice coincides with what you were taught was naughty.

Hairy Mary The opposite of a shaven haven.

Headache A pain in the neck.

Hide the sausage Infantile term for the act of sexual intercourse.

Horizontal jogging Unimaginative sexual intercourse.

Horses Mrs Patrick Campbell, the actress friend of George Bernard Shaw, advised: 'It doesn't matter what you do in the bedroom provided you don't do it in the streets and frighten the horses.'

Justin Trousersnake Nickname for priapic singer and rapper who goes by the official name of Timberlake.

Love bite Adolescent tattoo of affection, often lasting longer than the relationship.

Married sex Like going to the corner shop: there's not much variety, but it's always there (though special offers are rare).

Masochism The derivation of sexual pleasure from being controlled, humiliated or physically hurt by another person. Named after Leopold von Sacher-Masoch, a failed Austrian novelist who enjoyed being thrashed.

Masturbation In Woody Allen's words, 'It's sex with someone you love.'

Missionary The Genesis chapter one of sexual experimentation.

Necrophilia Sexual relations with a dead body. It is no defence to say that you couldn't tell because it didn't feel any different from usual.

No grass on the wicket Shaven haven (see overleaf).

Nymphomania Rare condition affecting women in which the sufferer is incapable of reaching a satisfying climax but is continually driven to do so by a high libido. Accounts of the happy nympho variety tend to be the products of immature male minds.

Onanism Posh word for masturbation.

Oral contraception Saying 'No'.

Paddle An implement which looks not unlike a small cricket bat, generally made from wood. Frequently the preferred means of chastisement in a bout of erotic spanking.

Pornography Anything, anywhere, considered obscene by someone, somewhere.

Roses Offering sent by a man to a woman shortly before, soon after, or occasionally instead of, a good night out. (*See* also 'Guilt'.)

Sadism The derivation of sexual pleasure from the infliction of pain or humiliation on another person. Named after the Marquis de Sade, a rich French sociopath who spent much of his life in jail. Despite copious writings on his alleged propensities he was only ever found guilty of two minor offences involving sexual violence. His favourite breakfast was a plain omelette served on a woman's buttocks and eaten with a sharp fork.

Satyriasis The male equivalent of nymphomania. The sufferer is taunted by an insatiable libido and never achieves true orgasmic relief.

Sexorcism Having casual sex with someone new to get over an ex.

Shaven haven A newly mowed lady lawn. The opposite of a Hairy Mary.

Sinners Those who transgress state-of-the-art morality.

Tantric sex Oriental art of prolonging passion to connect with your lover on a more spiritual plane. Most usually practised with a desire for longer orgasm, and occasionally from a desire to emulate once quite-cool singer Sting.

Ugandan discussions A term coined by the satirical magazine *Private Eye* to describe the act of hiding the sausage.

Viagra Erectile dysfunction wonder drug that does the biological equivalent of putting a sturdy flag pole on a clapped-out old building.

Voyeurism Gaining sexual pleasure from watching naked bodies or sexual activity. More impressively known as scopophilia.

Wank The name of a mountain in southern Germany, close to the Austrian border. Local residents have joined with the nearby Austrian village of Fucking and the Swiss community of Cunter to discuss how they might capitalise on the branding potential of their unusual names.

A BIT MORE BLUFFING...

Bluffer's GUIDE TO BREXIT

Bluffer's GUIDE TO CRICKET

Bluffer's GUIDE TO MANAGEMENT

Bluffer's GUIDE TO CYCLING

Bluffer's GUIDE TO SOCIAL MEDIA

Bluffer's GUIDE TO ETIQUETTE

Bluffer's GUIDE TO RACING

Bluffer's GUIDE TO GOLF

Bluffer's GUIDE TO WINE

Bluffer's GUIDE TO JAZZ

Bluffer's GUIDE TO DOGS

Bluffer's GUIDE TO FISHING

Bluffer's GUIDE TO OPERA

Bluffer's GUIDE TO CHOCOLATE

Bluffer's GUIDE TO CATS

Bluffer's GUIDE TO BEER

Bluffer's GUIDE TO QUANTUM UNIVERSE

Bluffer's GUIDE TO FOOTBALL

Bluffer's GUIDE TO RUGBY

Bluffer's GUIDE TO SKIING

Available from all good bookshops

bluffers.com